D0231841

A 1940s
Childhood

A 1940s Childhood

From Bomb Sites to
Children's Hour

JAMES MARSH

Cover illustration: Children in Kent during the big freeze of 1946–47. (War and Peace Archives)

First published 2014

The History Press
The Mill, Brimscombe Port
Stroud, Gloucestershire, GL5 2QG
www.thehistorypress.co.uk

© James Marsh, 2014

British Library Cataloguing in Publication Data.
A catalogue record for this book is available from the British Library.

ISBN 978 0 7524 9950 5

Typesetting and origination by The History Press
Printed in Great Britain

CONTENTS

FOREWORD

If, like me, you grew up in the 1940s, this book is the nearest thing to a time machine you are likely to experience. The boy's-eye view of these formative years awakens memories I hadn't expected to retain. Images from way back have flooded in: hunting for shrapnel after an air raid; eating toast thick with dripping; swatting flies that had somehow escaped the flypapers hanging from the ceiling; and singing 'There'll always be an England' at the riotous Saturday morning pictures. For our parents these were stressful years. Quite apart from the separations caused by war service and the shortages and deprivations, there was the threat of being bombed and invaded. But for most children, the war and its aftermath were opportunities for excitement and adventure. James Marsh perfectly captures this mood. What a good idea it is to view the decade from a child's perspective. I suppose we all tend to remember the positives. After my family was bombed out by a doodlebug in 1944 and we were homeless, I can recall the adventure of being billeted to a Cornish farm at harvest time, followed by the sense of importance it gave me when I eventually returned to my suburban school. I also remember the kindness of the Yankee GIs, who put on a Christmas party at the local base for kids like us. Only much later did I understand the trauma that the bombing must have been for my parents.

Even the enforced austerity of the post-war years didn't drag us down. School dinners were a bad joke we all shared. Our education was often rote learning enforced by the cane, but we had our ways of cheeking the teachers. The onset of smog was a chance to go home early and get lost on the way. Books looked dull and lacked jackets, but what a treat they gave our imaginations. James mentions Richmal Crompton's 'Just William' series, and I am sure my relish for those beautifully written books gave me a grounding in the language that later enabled me to take up writing as a career. But I mustn't be tempted to pick out my favourites – it's done so much more eloquently in the pages that follow.

Peter Lovesey

ACKNOWLEDGEMENTS

I have to thank the following people for the time they took to tell me their childhood stories and for the help I received in putting this book together: Penny Legg, for all her help and advice that did so much to bring this book to fruition; Joe Legg, Penny's husband, who was there for me and was a huge help in transporting me to 1940s shows; Thomas and Joe Legg, for all of their help with the shows and the photographs of the London Underground; Jim Brown, for the excerpts from his books about policing in the 1940s; Peter and Jax Lovesey, for the wonderful foreword for the book and their fascinating memories of school life; James Reeves, for editing the manuscript; Julie Green, always a big help with photographs of old Southampton; Nigel Smith; Sophia Brothers; Martin Longhurst, for his input about childhood in Portsmouth; Keith and Gloria Tordoff, of the Oldest Sweet Shop in England; Kirsty Shepherd, the Oldest Sweet Shop in England; James Noyce, British Pathé;

Melanie Sambells, Mirrorpix; Simon Murray, London Transport Museum; Anna Renton, London Transport Museum; Joe D'Cruz, Getty Images; John and Mel Sions and family, for their family photographs taken at Brooklands Museum; C Carte, Tram 57 project, that produced the great photos of trams in Southampton; Dame Vera Lynn, for permission to mention her in the book; Anita Nimmo, for setting this up with Dame Vera – my appreciation goes to her for this; Ian Dawson, alias Viv the Spiv, for his help and co-operation; Bill Fowler, The War and Peace Show; The Home Front Bus, War and Peace Show; Eddie Cambers, The Home Front Bus; Ian Bayley, 1940s Society; Rex Cadman, The War and Peace Show; Roger Smoothy, Kent photographic archives; and Lesley Maxim, Romney, Hythe and Dimchurch Railway.

INTRODUCTION

When I was asked to write this book it was the answer to something I had wanted to do for some time. I had already published my own story of being born in Southampton in 1940 and growing up there during and after the Second World War, but I quickly realised this was only a small part of the whole story. Great Britain was bombed severely during that conflict, so children across the country went through the same trials and hardships. I knew this and wanted to get this message out if I could. Then came the offer of writing *A 1940s Childhood: From Bombsites to Children's Hour*. Now my chance had come to write a child's view of the most devastating decade in this country's history. I have enjoyed every moment of the time it took me to accomplish this. IA lot of people shared their memories of childhood in the 1940s with me, and this has given me the chance to give the children of Great Britain a voice and show the war from their viewpoint.

One thing shines through it all and that is the fact that kids will be kids, no matter what is happening in the world around them. I hope I have captured that very important point in this book.

James Marsh, 2014

One

A Decade of Challenge

September 1940. You should be tucked up warm and snug in your bed. Mum will start shouting for you to get up soon because it's a school day. But there's more than one mum shouting this morning. You're not in your own bed, or even your own home. This is the platform of Piccadilly Circus Underground station, where you were rushed last night because of the air raid that took place before bedtime. We've had to put up with this sort of thing ever since our Prime Minister, Mr Chamberlain, told the whole country we were at war with Germany. Boys and girls everywhere will remember the broadcast, sitting around the wireless on that Sunday morning:

**THIS STATION
WILL NOW REMAIN
OPEN
DURING AIR RAID
ALERTS**

LONDON ⊖ TRANSPORT

It soon became apparent that the Underground was the safest place for London people to shelter from the constant bombing of the capital. (London Transport Museum)

This morning the British Ambassador in Berlin handed the German Government a final Note stating that, unless we heard from them by 11 o'clock that they were prepared at once to withdraw their troops from Poland, a state of war would exist between us. I have to tell you now that no such undertaking has been received, and that consequently this country is at war with Germany.

Children received this news with a mixture of excitement and fear. The world we knew, both school and home life, would change beyond all recognition. Some were already being sent to safer places to get away from the bombing. Towns and cities around our country were supplying gas masks and strangely named things like Anderson shelters. First of all I helped dad. Then he went away, to fight, according to mum, so I helped granddad dig a blooming great hole in the back garden for these to be put up. And for what? Well, ever since that man your mum calls Adolf Hitler started having his aeroplanes drop bombs on us, we need somewhere to get safely away and hopefully stay alive. Here in London most of us rush down to the Underground and spend the night there. It's okay really because there's a lot of fun to be had as you race your mates along the platforms making plane noises. But the grown-ups don't like it and tell us to pipe down all the time. Where's their sense of adventure?

Children everywhere are coping well, even the ones who emerge from wherever they are sheltering (Underground stations, Anderson shelters in back gardens, strong brick shelters in roads and parks all over Great Britain) to find their houses reduced to rubble. It's not only family possessions that are gone, but all of your toys as well. Imagine your horror at finding not only toy soldiers crushed and melted, but your precious toy cars as well. Some had models of Spitfires and even some of Great Britain's amazing battleships, the mighty *Hood*, the *Prince of Wales* and the *Rodney* taking pride of place in most collections. The German Navy had better watch out when those ships start fighting with them. In later months news starts to come in from all over the country of towns and cities that have been bombed. That man Adolf Hitler claims he and his armies are soon going to invade England; the cheeky blighter says he is going to take over Buckingham Palace. No fear, he certainly won't ever get anywhere near there. Our troops will stop him, you'll see.

Coming up from the Underground into the daylight, it's embarrassing to have to hold your mum's hand. After all you're nearly grown up now and can certainly look after yourself. This war, that we were told would be over by Christmas, is getting far more serious, so mum holds on to you as you made your way home. The question is, will your home still be there?

If not, then the civil defence blokes will tell us to go down the church hall, where bombed-out families are being given tea, blankets and stuff like that. Arrangements will then be made for re-homing. This usually means moving in with relatives.

News coming in on the wireless is making the grown-ups very angry and upset. Towns and cities have been badly damaged again by the Germans. Coventry is the one most of them are talking about. It was hit by

All that is now left of the once magnificent cathedral in Coventry. It was destroyed along with much of the city in a devastating raid by German planes in 1940. (Penny Legg)

such a big air raid on the night of 14 November 1940 that the whole place was reduced almost to rubble. Children can't even imagine what this must have been like, because they haven't the understanding their parents have. After all, their own city or town was also hit and a lot of houses have been bombed. There are ruins all over the place, and in some areas German bomber planes were shot down by our men. What a lot of fun can be had with these, if you can get anywhere near one. Souvenirs from a shot-down German plane are priceless. What if you could handle one of the machine guns, or even get a piece of one? Just a tiny bit with German writing on would make you king in your playground when you showed it around. But first you need to get near, and that was something us children very rarely get the chance to do because the wreckage is guarded so closely by those civil defence blokes, the local police and the army. But shrapnel, found lying all over the place in the days after an air raid, quickly finds its way into short trouser pockets of boys as they make their way to school, carrying their gas masks in cardboard boxes slung over their shoulders. Sometimes you can find bullets as well, which have come either from German planes or our own guns that are shooting back. Though it's great in the morning doing this on the way to school, those who stay in their own homes and hide under the stairs during a night-time air raid just cower in fear as they hear the bombs falling.

It is during the Battle of Britain that the new Prime Minister, Winston Churchill, who took over from Mr Chamberlain on the 10 May 1940, says of our air force pilots: 'Never in the field of human conflict has so much been owed by so many to so few.' This was to become such a famous phrase that our pilots would be known as 'the few' from then on. Spitfires and Hurricanes are fast and adaptable, so are

At the 1940s Show at Brooklands Museum in Weybridge, Surrey, these children look just as their counterparts during the war did. Both are dressed in 1940s clothes and their gas mask cases are clearly in view. (Author)

able to account for many German aircraft in the skies above Great Britain. They are called upon so many times to scramble and take to the air as more and more German raiders approach, wanting to destroy our Royal Air Force on the ground and in so doing take control of the skies above us. Then the German troops would be able to make their way across the English Channel and occupy our wonderful country.

Pooh, they'll never get a chance to do that, will they? Haven't our schoolteachers told us so many times that British is best? Our soldiers, sailors and airmen will soon put a stop to their little game – at least that's what your mum keeps telling you as well. Children all over England have to practice putting on the gas masks that were issued in case the Germans started to use the mustard gas they used against our troops in the First World War (1914–18).

What a farce this is. The boys did it fine, but the girls have all sorts of trouble pulling them over the carefully made up hair that their mothers seem to spend so much time brushing and styling for them. All the boys have to do is put a comb through theirs every morning before starting off for school. Not for them the shoulder-length, carefully brushed hair-styles, just a very simple short back and sides. That's if you're lucky enough to be taken to the barber's, to sit on a plank put across the chair so you're high enough for him to cut your hair properly. The alternative is having your mum or granddad doing it, and if this happens you end up with a basin cut. A pudding basin is plonked on your head and any hair showing beneath is cut off as neatly as possible. At any other time, boys who went to school with this cut would be ridiculed unmercifully by their schoolmates. But this decade is so different from any other, as the war rages on and more and more houses and business premises are wrecked by German bombs. There is much more to take up the interest of children, so something as trivial as a basin haircut quickly passed down the ladder of things to wonder and laugh at.

At home and school, children have to practise getting into air-raid shelters as soon as the sirens sound. Leaving everything you were doing at once, it is single file and walk as quickly as you can to get to the relative safety. At home, in towns and cities outside of London, it is to the bottom of the garden or the big shelters outside in the roads. But at school this usually means going underground into the cellars where the school equipment is stored. Everywhere, too, kids help their mums and teachers stick brown tape crosswise over the glass of all the windows. This is to prevent bomb blast injury; any shattering glass will be caught up in the sticky tape instead of flying all over the place.

Some boys, who were getting used to these raids, start counting as the bombs impact on the ground. They know these are dropped in sticks of eight at a time. So if eight explosions sound, then that lot of bombs has at least missed the spot where you are sheltering.

Families have to bring everything of utmost importance with them to the shelters, and high on this list are ration books. Issued in 1939, every family has to have these in order to buy anything needed for their own use. Food, clothing, and household requirements are only available when accompanied by coupons taken from these books. There are different colours for different things: grey for food, red for clothing etc. It is necessary to do things in this way because Great Britain is already very short of everything its citizens need on a daily basis. Our ships are being unmercifully torpedoed and sunk by German submarines (U-boats). Other merchant ships are quickly being commandeered to help in this situation, which means things like bananas disappearing from our shops because they are non-essential. That man Hitler – he thinks that if he sinks all of our merchant ships Britain will starve and have to make peace with him as a result. He doesn't know us at all. We can take anything he dishes out. Sitting down to breakfast before going to school with bread and dripping to eat isn't so bad, but the powdered milk and eggs your mum is now buying – urgh!

'Eat it up, it's just as good as the milk and eggs we had before the war, it's just powdered to make it go

These children are waiting to be evacuated from their homes in Kent. Their belongings can clearly be seen, as can the labels pinned to the front of their clothes. (War and Peace Archives)

further,' is what your mum tells you. None of the children agree with that. How can anything be made to taste so awful?

Some boys and girls, well a lot actually, are sent to safer places to get away from the bombing. They are lucky in many ways – not having to eat this powdered stuff, for a start. But they do have to suffer separation from homes and families. They turn up at the railway stations in all the big towns and cities with gas masks and labels pinned to their coats with their names on. What is that like? Saying goodbye to your mum, and probably your gran as well, then watching them disappear as the train pulls out of the station. Where is it going? What will happen to you now? For them, though, in many cases it is to a life free from the fear of bombs and with more food available, the lucky ones ending up on farms with the joy of seeing animals and going to small country schools. There, many of them do things city kids never even thought about: country dancing, fishing and swimming in idyllic country rivers and streams.

Dunkirk

Dunkirk really showed that Hitler bloke what our men are made of. His army trapped our forces on the beaches of a French place with an unusual name, Dunkirk. Well we wouldn't let him do that for long would we? Wasn't our new prime minister, Mr Churchill, telling us, 'we will fight them on the beaches'? Well that's exactly what we are doing, even if it is in a foreign country. Mums and grannies have their own ideas about this: 'You can fight on the beaches if you want to mate, but you won't catch us doing that.'

Then, what news! It's all round the playground at school. On 26–27 May 1940 the great evacuation of British and French troops begins. Hooray! The British Navy, our air force, then a whole load of small boats go over there and bring our men home, along with some French ones. It won't take our troops long to get back into the fight – then you had better look out, Mr Hitler!

New Playgrounds

With bombing a regular occurrence, boys are soon taking advantage of new playgrounds. Here is the chance to have your very own headquarters in what was once someone's home. Furniture that was more or less still intact can be used, and camps and secret hide-outs are springing up all over the country. The families who lived here before they were bombed don't think it is so great but what joy it is for us. They can become a cowboy sheriff's office or anything you want it to be. Adventure all the way. Girls come in sometimes, though. How do they do that? Boys don't do the same things as them, like skipping or playing with dolls. They takeover and want to play houses, and mothers and fathers. They tidy up and stuff like that.

Although things like Bonfire Night and sporting activities have been cancelled, children who live in villages outside of some of the major towns and cities can still enjoy the wonder of fireworks. The Germans don't drop bombs on these places, which is why so many have been evacuated to them. But looking out through holes in the blackout curtains at night, as long as there isn't a light on in the room, it's possible to see searchlights probing the skies and bombs going off when they land. This is so thrilling that it's like having Bonfire Night every night of the week.

In early 1940, parts of the London are bombed and set on fire. There are stories of boys and girls thrilling to the sight of the horizon lit up in red every night as the fires raged. It is just like firework night for them and they enjoy a cup of cocoa as they watch this spectacle. But as the bombing moves ever closer to where they are living the nightly display is no longer something to wonder at; the danger becomes all too clear. So no more watching the flames leaping skywards and, alas, no more cocoa either.

Boys mainly still have the job of collecting old newspaper and such. Well we are all experts at this, but instead of it being once a year starting in September for the 'bommie' it is now an all-year-round thing. This waste paper, along with anything metal, old saucepans, small tin baths and anything else us eager beavers can get our hands on, is horded until there's enough to be collected for the war effort. If there's enough, the ones who have collected the most are rewarded with chocolate. Keeping girls away from this activity and the rewards it can bring is not easy to do. They argue that they're just as good at this as boys, and who can really argue with that? Even mums tell us the girls should be involved because this war affects us all. Well, what can you say to that? Most boys still think girls should be playing with their dolls or helping their mums in the house. They do this all the time and help with the shopping as well. After all, that's what girls are supposed to do, they are told. Not be out in the roads picking up things like shrapnel, cigarette packets and matchboxes. Things found on the ground are dirty, so let the boys do that. Girls must stay clean and help their mums as much as they can.

And what about sport? Wolverhampton Wanderers get to the Cup Final at Wembley in 1939 and play against Portsmouth. This southern team has done well to get to the final, but surely they have no chance against Wolves who, along with the national side, are captained by the great Stan Cullis. The result is a shock to the whole country. Portsmouth 4, Wolves 1. That's not what anyone expected. Portsmouth's goals were scored by Bert Barlow, John Anderson and two by Cliff Parker. Wolves' goal came from Dicky Dorsett. After that the flipping war starts, and football, along with all other sports, is discontinued. The team that sprung such a surprise on the best in the country and won the FA Cup is holding on to it, and will do so until the war is over.

The *Hood* and the *Bismarck*

Then comes news that our most famous battleship, the mighty *Hood*, has been blown up and sunk by a German battleship, the *Bismarck*, on 24 May 1941. What could possibly have gone wrong here? The *Hood* was indestructible. No ship afloat could possibly stand up to her. Your mum is telling you that the German ship just got lucky and caught her unawares. That must be true. The *Prince of Wales* was a brand new ship with workmen still aboard her, so once the *Hood* was sunk she couldn't fight that German ship on her own, could she? Especially since the *Bismarck* had another ship backing her up. It had a funny name, the *Prinz Eugen* – we can't even pronounce it (the prinz eeyoogen). Whoever thought up a name like that? But the *Bismarck* herself is sunk only a few days later on 27 May, when one of our swordfish planes hits her rudder with a torpedo. She can't steer, so our mighty Atlantic fleet catches up with her and blows her out of the water. Well, that's what they say on the wireless, anyway.

School

Kids aren't allowed to misbehave in school, and teachers are extremely strict in this respect. Even whispering in class means the cane descending on hands with such force as to leave a bright red weal. But when news of the sinking of the *Bismarck* is given, boys especially jump up on to their desks and leap up and down in glee shouting, 'Yeah, we got them, our navy's the best in the blooming world.' Teachers, almost as excited as their pupils at this great news, simply smile and look on as this gleeful behaviour takes place.

Usually this kind of thing would be a million miles away from happening in any school, discipline is so strict. It is nothing for a teacher to bring out a cane and swish it through the air before crashing it down on his desk. This lets everyone in the class know that he means business and that any misbehaviour will result in that cane coming down with painful force on to unprotected hands. Some boys, of course, try to bluff this out by showing the teacher and the rest of the class that this was nothing to them, the girls especially being targeted for this display. It is hard to do though, because you can only bluff so much. When both your hands are stinging to such an extent that you want to cry out, keeping a couldn't-care-less smile on your face is something of an achievement.

Sometimes the war helps a lot in this direction – like if you are lucky enough to turn up for school to find all the other children dancing in glee in the play-ground shouting, 'Thank you, Adolf.' Behind them, on these occasions, is a smoking ruin that only the day before was their school. Because the attack came at night, no one was in the building at the time, not even the ancient old caretaker, whom all the kids know, of course. An unexpected holiday now takes place while they try to find us different schools. 'Take your time,' is the chant. Girls skip in the roads among the ruined houses. Boys occupy the camps set up in within them or are out on the big shrapnel hunt.

Sometimes boys are delighted to find bullets that have dropped from the planes. Live ammunition, whether German or British, is a wonder and a joy to find. It is also very dangerous, though, and any adult who sees you with it quickly takes it away. If you can find them, though, it is the greatest fun setting the bullets off. The trick is to anchor them where they will be held firmly, then take a rock and bash the end with that. No one has a gun of course, so this is the only way to get it to fire. It is important to watch where you were standing when someone was bashing the bullet. Many a boy has his hair parted with a big bang and the bullet flying just as it would have done out of the barrel of a real gun. A hair parting is funny, but just a bit lower and it could be very dangerous and even fatal.

Bomb Disposal

Bombs hit the ground but don't always go off. This means the very brave soldiers of the disposal units have to come in and defuse them. Whole roads are closed while waiting for the shout of 'All clear!' The explosive device has hopefully been safely taken care of. Sadly, though, sometimes it isn't a shout we hear but a great explosion when the bomb does go off. Many of our brave men are killed like that.

Rationing

With this war going on, it is exciting and frightening all at the same time. But the worst thing for all of us is being rationed. Mums have become geniuses where cooking is concerned. Powdered milk and eggs we know about, but just how mum manages to produce such lovely stews and puddings on meagre rations is nothing short of a miracle. Girls, of course, smirk at the boys because they help their mums, so they know what goes into these things. Boys, however, are blissfully unaware of what they are actually eating, and in some cases that is just as well!

Vegetables are grown in most gardens, so they are available a lot of the time. Most mums now give things like rhubarb to their kids, who wouldn't normally like it. Boys especially are not partial to this, or indeed any vegetables. But when there isn't anything else to eat then whatever mum puts on the table is okay with us. And really, stew made with only vegetables isn't all that bad, as long as mum uses a lot of gravy powder. The fact that there isn't any meat in it is covered up by that. Cottage pie is made the same way, with lots of gravy at the bottom of the dish and loads of mashed potato on top. Then if there is any cheese this goes on as well. It comes down to the fact that if you don't want to eat what mum puts up she'll just say, 'Right then, go without.' That always does it, because we need food, don't we?

Potatoes and some fruits are not on ration, but mum has to be quick to get to whatever shop she's registered at if she has any chance of getting oranges. We are being told they are only for children and pregnant women.

Clothes are also getting harder to come by. Not only are they rationed, shortages mean the prices are going up, so these days it's mostly handed-downs we are wearing. Now the country is at war, nothing is wasted. Hitler is doing his best to make sure the things we need to survive are being sent to the bottom of the Atlantic, so everyone is saying, 'If there's still wear in them then someone can get the benefit.'

Walking to school wearing a shirt and trousers that some other boy has grown out of is something we all have to get used to. Not even the girls get away with this; they are also being given clothes discarded by older children. But of course, as mum says, there's always old Mr Fryer. He can help when the rations are low, or the queues at the shops get too long and the stuff the ladies are waiting to buy runs out before they can get to the front. These men are getting stuff from somewhere called the black market. None of us know where that is and mum is always saying we have to be careful when we shop with Mr Fryer.

'We don't use the ration books you see,' she says. 'So if anyone finds out he will get into trouble.' Most roads in towns all over England have their own Mr Fryer, selling things you can't get in any of the shops. And there were always people like 'Viv the Spiv'. Men like him in most big cities can get anything you want without ever needing coupons for them. The black market again – we really ought to be able to find out where this is. With watches going right up their arms, they sell these to whoever can afford them. Everything they do is against the law, but so many mums are grateful to them for supplying this very essential service.

We hear stories from our mums and sisters about these men and how they avoid getting into trouble: bottles of whiskey are hidden in dolls' prams. If the police or ARP wardens stop the men and demand to know why they were out so late, they are told,

'It's alright, I'm just collecting my daughter from my sister's house and getting her home.' Cigarettes are hidden in ladies' beds – of course, she has the measles so the bed can't be searched. Mats are put on to floors to cover up the suspicious holes the size of pennies or shillings in the lino. These cut out pieces of lino are then used in the electricity and gas meters. For all of us these things are such a laugh because we don't see that it is wrong at all.

Onions, butter, and even in some cases real nylon stockings, are the things to go to Mr Fryer or 'Viv the Spiv' for. Why do big sisters make such a fuss about nylons? If there aren't any they can get their hands on it's a laugh to see them drawing a line down the back of their legs to look like the seam of a pair of these stockings.

Then, on the wireless, comes news of the raid by Japan on somewhere called Pearl Harbor in Hawaii. Where's that? We all want to know. Anyway, mums and grannies are pleased. Teachers are telling us so many American sailors were killed in the attack that their President Roosevelt has told our Mr Churchill that they are now coming into the war to help fight the Germans as well as the Japanese.

This is great news, but also confusing. American soldiers are coming over here and they're called 'Gee Eyes'. Your big sisters are really happy because these Americans have things we can't get now. They have real stockings for a start. And what is this dance they're all raving about? These American blokes have brought over jitterbugging with them. What's that? Are they scared of bugs and are jumping about all over the place because it's giving them the jitters?

The ladies are welcome to their stockings. Boys and girls know these Gee Eye soldiers also have what we crave, and that is sweets. The ones in our shops are all on ration and the price has gone up since the war started. 'Profiteering', mum calls it. We haven't a clue what that means. We just have to work harder in our spare time to earn as much pocket money as possible, then learn to make the ration coupons go round so they last until we get the next lot.

But all of us know just what to do when we see American soldiers. The cry goes up every time. 'Got any gum, chum?' It always works, and we sit in our camps on the bits of furniture we've saved and really enjoy this treat. For children whose homes have been bombed the American GIs give parties, and these are absolutely great. Deprived kids are given chocolate bars with a funny name, 'hershee bars' (Hershey bars), and there are people giving shows, like conjurers and stuff. There is always a Laurel and Hardy film to watch and laugh at as well.

The raids are being kept up night after night, which means in the daytime there are all sorts of things that can be done. Boys, for instance, can stand on top of the rubble of ruined houses and launch themselves by means of ropes tied to lamp posts, taking off and swinging round and round until landing back on their feet again. Girls still manage to skip and play at hopscotch. Even amongst the bomb damage they string a rope across the street and skip all at the same time.

All the main cities in England, Scotland and Wales are suffering. London has it worst with air raids every night. Blimey, even Buckingham Palace has been hit. But it's bad in other places. In Scotland, Edinburgh, Glasgow and the Clyde are getting it worst because of the shipyards. And in places like Manchester, Liverpool and Bolton – anywhere there are docks or mills – the bombs keep falling.

In the Underground stations it isn't so bad, because we now have hammocks strung across the tracks and lots of us sleep in them. It's smashing and really comfortable, although many of us are frightened an Underground train will come racing into the station while we're asleep. Mum tells us this can't happen because the electric current is turned off at night, and we're all up before it's turned on again in the morning.

El Alamein

We're getting pretty fed up with being bombed all the time. A lot of us are wondering when we are going to bash the Germans back for the way they keep hitting us. The answer to this comes in October 1942. It's on the wireless. British forces under the command of Field Marshal Montgomery (Monty to all of us), known as the desert rats, are fighting at somewhere called El Alamein and they are making good progress against the enemy, who are under the command of Field Marshal Erwin Rommel, the desert fox.

We've all heard of him, haven't we? Our teachers have told us he's the best they've got, and our forces seem to think he's unbeatable. But twelve days later, on 4 November, the news comes through. Rommel has been beaten back and our men, led on by Monty, are driving him and his Afrika Korps out of the desert. We don't know how important this is of course, because we don't even know where the desert is, let alone somewhere with a name like El Alamein. But it's a great victory for us. We told that Mr Adolf Hitler we'd beat him, didn't we? On the wireless Mr Churchill is saying something we again don't really understand: 'Now this is not the end. It is not even the beginning of the end. But it is, perhaps, the end of the beginning.' We're all content just to shout 'hooray!'

D–Day and the Doodlebugs

France, Belgium, Holland and other places have been occupied by our enemies for a long time. It is 6 June 1944 and our men are setting off to push those Germans out. Some children have come over here to live with us, because it's not good when your home country has been overrun by foreign soldiers. Mums everywhere are getting excited because our men are waiting to board ships that will sail from places like Southampton across the English Channel. In school we're being told that our men, as well as our allies, the Americans and other soldiers fighting with us, will land on specially picked beaches in Normandy. Watch out, Mr Hitler, because once we get there we'll fight you all the way back to your own country.

It's so exciting when these ships set out. Our teachers are calling this a huge flotilla, the biggest ever to sail, and it does so in the worst storm in the Channel for years. It is a big success, although a lot of our men are killed due to beachheads being established. They have their own landing equipment, so men, trucks and tanks can be lowered on to them and simply driven ashore.

So how can Mr Hitler have any hope of winning now? Mums and grannies are excited and are saying that the end of the war is now near. The bombing isn't anywhere near as bad because we've shot down so many of their planes. Surely we can start to relax a bit and simply wait for it to be over?

But in London there's a nasty shock waiting. It is so bad that some children who have been there with their parents throughout all the bombing are now being evacuated, like so many before them. It's because of what our mums are calling doodlebugs (V1s). Our men who work on the anti-aircraft guns are trying to shoot these things down and they have got some, but the ones that get through are awesome. With no pilots, they are driven by jet propulsion (that's what our teachers tell us anyway). They are shot up a ramp, and a jet engine drives them until they get over London, then it gives out and they just drop, and boy do they explode when they hit the ground. A new fear is gripping us all; these doodlebugs are such a threat. Mr Churchill knows this, so the War Cabinet is brought in to try and find a solution. What is this cabinet and where do they keep it? All the grown-ups are talking about this threat, night and day. The horrible noise these flying bombs make is bad enough, but when the engine cuts out there's just a swishing sound as they drop. No one knows where the doodlebug will land until the huge explosion happens.

Our men are pushing on through Europe, so it can't be long before it's over. A pity, really, because a lot of boys have smashing collections of shrapnel. Once the war ends so will our supplies. It's bad enough that chewing gum disappeared when the American soldiers went away on D-Day, but the thrill of finding interesting shrapnel has become something of an art. Paperboys are fortunate because they go out early in the morning on their rounds and so they have the pick after the previous night's air raid.

You have to be careful in case what you have picked up is dangerous. Some boys come across unexploded bombs – incendiaries, they call them – and are over-joyed to find them. Things like this make them kings in their school playgrounds. But the grown-ups aren't nearly so pleased when their sons carry these trophies home. They are very quickly confiscated and taken to the nearest police station, where they are put in buckets of sand. All the way home the poor boy who found it is told off by his mum:

'Don't you ever bring anything as dangerous as this home again. You would have been killed if it had gone off. And we would have been as well if it went off in the house. Don't your teachers tell you not to go anywhere near anything as dangerous as an incen-diary bomb?'

'Yeah, they do, but how are we to know what they are when we don't even know what they flipping look like?'

We hear of one lad called Ed Chambers from Aldgate in the East End of London. He was only 5 when he was at home with his granddad on 21 October 1940.

A bomb exploded in the street outside the house and blew the front right in. His granddad was killed but little Ed was saved by the table he was under, though he still had to be dug out from the rubble. When they got him out it was found he had shrapnel stuck in his left arm, from the shoulder right down to his elbow. Well that's one way of getting shrapnel, I suppose, but that young boy wouldn't agree with any of us about that. Even we know how frightened and hurt he must have been, and we think he is quite a hero.

Now it's May 1945 and the grown-ups are going mad, jumping up and down and dancing in the streets. They're all shouting, 'It's over, the war's over!' Trafalgar Square in London is packed and our Mr Churchill is waving and holding up two fingers, a sign that means victory. The Germans have surrendered and we've won the war. Down come the blackout curtains, and bonfires are prepared in many roads. Small children are given anything that will make a noise when banged, like a saucepan or tin tray. Before, nothing that would help the enemy was allowed, so showing a light or making any sort of noise was strictly forbidden.

But this doesn't matter any more. It's all over and we've won, so small children are now having a whale of a time, running up and down, and making a fearful noise with their pots and pans. The blackout curtains make a super 'bommie', which is lit as soon as it's dark enough on this wonderful day. For the first time in five and a half years children are thrilling to the sight of fire lighting up the areas all around it. It's Bonfire Night again, although we haven't got any fireworks. Life as we knew it before this man Hitler caused so much trouble for us can now start getting back to the way it was, and everyone will be pleased about that.

The Anderson shelters in the gardens can now be got rid of, though a lot of women have done wonders with these during the war years. Growing your own food was a neat way to avoid the shortages so soil was placed on the roofs and they were planted with vegetables for the families to eat. Why stop now? Home-grown vegetables, rabbit, and eggs from chickens (which also provide a smashing dinner at Christmas) can be made into either stews or pies, and help so much. Mothers now don't have to get to the shops they are registered at quite so often for meat and vegetables. For other groceries they still have to queue for a long time in the hope that the shop will still have things left to sell by the time they get to the front. The practice of growing your own was carried on in gardens all over the country, while dads and granddads used the inside of the shelters as garden sheds – they were just right for this.

Who is this Man?

many children born at the very start of the Second World War had rarely got to see their dads. They were in the armed forces and busy fighting the Germans. They seldom, if ever, got home leave, so these children were growing up not knowing anything about them.

As 1946 arrives, so too do many servicemen who have survived. They do something called demob, and then simply come home again. Many of them find that the house they left no longer exists, and their families are now living in places they had been allocated. For some this means Nissan huts, which the American forces used to live in while they were over here with us.

Some families are being moved into hastily erected houses called prefabs (prefabricated housing) and boy are they the lucky ones. This sort of house is only meant to last a few years, until replacements can be built for the ones that have been bombed. But for families moving into these, life is suddenly a lot better than anything they knew before the war. Gone is the need for mums to heat water in the gas boiler in the kitchen to fill up the tin bath, which hangs on the wall outside, next to the outdoor toilet. Prefabs have an indoor bathroom, complete with bathtub and a water heater. This is smashing; just turn on the water, fill up the bath, then when you've finished pull out the plug and the water goes away. It's as easy as that, though mums keep on at you to clean the bath as the water drains out. 'Swish it around as it runs out,' they shout, 'that way we won't have a grimy ring around the bath. No one wants to use it if you leave your dirty tidemark do they?'

Ah well, this is progress I suppose. Things like tide-marks were never mentioned when you finished bathing in the kitchen in the tin baths. It was just carried outside and the water tipped down the outside drain. It was awkward doing this, as the water swished about a lot. Once an end was put on the ground it was okay though, to just tip the bath up and watch the water rushing away. Some boys weren't really strong enough to carry their end of the bath and more than one ended up dropping it before they reached the drain. When this happened the person at the other end (usually your mum) couldn't hold on and the bath tipped up, sending the water over the unfortunate boy. Many a mum ended up in fits of laughter as they looked at their sons, now soaked to the skin and not at all happy. But with an indoor bath this carrying chore has ended.

The prefabs also have a very modern-looking kitchen, and something that before the war was a luxury that only well-off people could afford to have: a refrigerator. It is out of this world. Mum can keep things like milk, butter (when she can get some) and our small weekly ration of bacon in here and it stays cold and fresh. There was no more need for the home-made larder called a meat safe that had to be placed away from direct sunlight.

Whether their families were in their old house or in a new prefab, fathers are coming home to a mixed reception. Kids who were around 5 or 6 when the war started can still remember the man they called a dad before he went away to fight. But the younger ones don't have a clue who this stranger is who has suddenly turned up in their homes.

Every house (except the posh ones) can only afford to have one fire burning, usually in the parlour. This is where the whole family lives throughout the cold winter months. Mums get up much earlier than anyone else to clean yesterday's ashes out of the grate, and carry these out to the dustbin before lighting today's fire. If more than one boy lives there it is common practice to race each other downstairs, with the winner getting the chair nearest the fire – and grinning at his brothers as they struggle into their clothes away from its warmth. Suddenly, though, this race is stopped as young boys gaze in horror at a giant of a man who is now occupying their coveted fireside chair. For smaller boys this is a frightening experience. Aren't grown-ups always telling us to beware of strangers and never talk to them? So who is this one inside our home? Instinct takes over as both boys and girls take refuge behind their mother. Clinging to her dress they gaze out at the giant by the fire before being brought out into the open. Then in so many homes up and down the country they all hear the same reassurance: 'There's nothing to be afraid of, this is your father.' It's such a strange thing, holding out your small hand, which is entirely engulfed in the big one of the giant's, and shaking it, quietly say, 'How do you do.'

The school playground is alive because so many other children have experienced the same introduction to their father. Family they never even knew they had are suddenly turning up in their lives. Teachers are explaining it all and telling the ones who have gone through this how lucky they are. 'Your fathers have survived the war and come home,' they say. 'Many of our men didn't, so be proud and welcome your fathers home again.' In some cases this is smashing as you get to know your dad. But not all homes have it so lucky. These men have just fought a bitter war with a ruthless enemy. Now they are finding it hard to get used to being home again, some suffering paranoid visions brought about by the recent trauma. Sometimes we are woken up at night by dad shouting 'The enemy are surrounding us. Open fire,' or cowering under the stairs when a thunderstorm breaks, and mum just tells us not to worry, 'It's the war'.

Then, as we get into 1946, the children who were evacuated start coming home. They have been to the countryside and had a lot of fun, swimming in rivers and lakes, working on farms and seeing all the animals that town children never see. Now they're home again and looking at the place where they were born as it is now, smashed into rubble. Never mind, we'll soon educate them to the wonderful playgrounds we have and the fun that can be had in our camps. The war games we play as British soldiers, always, of course, getting the better of our German enemies.

The girls go on playing hopscotch and skipping, in roads where there are practically no houses undamaged. They practised rescuing people while the war was on, using dolls to represent people trapped in the rubble. Now, though, they can get back to playing properly. They make a good job of this, skipping with six or more doing it at the same time. Boys try it too, but the flipping rope keeps getting tangled around our feet so that we fall over. The girls think this is hilarious. Well, that's okay because skipping is a girl's game anyway.

Return of Sport

Sport is starting up again and first it's cricket. We have a series of Test matches against an Australian side, called the Victory Tests. They take place just after the war is over. But as England's team is at nearly at full strength and Australia's isn't, these matches are reduced to just county standard. It is great though, and the grounds are packed out. There are three matches played, each one over three days, and the result is one win each with the third one drawn. The first county championship gets under way and a Test series for England against India is also arranged. England wins this by winning the first Test match while the other two are drawn.

So now it's over to Australia for the Ashes to start again. We've got a good chance here. Our team is captained by the great batsman Wally Hammond. Also in the team are super players like Len Hutton, Denis Compton (who also plays football for Arsenal), Bill Edrich and our wicketkeeper Godfrey Evans. We'll show those Australians a thing or two and win back the Ashes. They've had them for long enough, it's only fair that we get them back this time. But they've still got Donald Bradman playing for them, and he alone is the reason we lose again.

Oh well, roll on the football season. Boy it's great to have this back. We love going to the grounds and cheering our team on while making a fearful noise with the rattles. As boys we are always put at the front of the crowds so we get a good view. We are handed down over the grown-ups heads and carried over a sea of flat caps until we reach the front. Our dads are somewhere at the back, but we know they'll find us alright at the end of the game and take us home safely.

Also, it's them who make sure the pies and cups of Bovril are given to us at half-time. It's just wonderful that the normal League games are being played again, but during the war some of our most famous players didn't want to have to stop playing altogether – Stanley Matthews, Nat Lofthouse, Stan Cullis and other well-known players from First Division sides turned out in friendly matches playing for teams in the area where they were stationed. What must it have been like when supporters of lower league teams saw such famous players in their colours?

In 1945, a team called Moscow Dynamo comes over to play games against two of our best First Division teams, Chelsea and Arsenal. This is exciting because they are a foreign team from a country called Russia. Our famous teams will soon show this foreign side how this great game of football should be played. After all, we're the best in the world at it, aren't we? A lot of us feel sorry for these players coming all this way to be beaten by our teams. Especially as Chelsea have the great Tommy Lawton playing for them. He could beat any side practically on his own. Then there's Arsenal, fielding two of this country's greatest players as well, Stanley Matthews and Stan Mortenson. What chance does any team have against them, we all want to know? The results shock us all. Chelsea only manage a draw against this Russian team, while Arsenal lose. Blimey, that's not possible is it?

The Arsenal game is played at Spurs' ground (White Hart Lane) and our dads tell us the only reason Arsenal lost was because of the fog. It was a real London pea-souper and even though we were, as usual, right at the front, all we could see of the players was the Russian goalkeeper. He had a funny name that amused us all so much. Tiger Komich. How can anyone be called Tiger? That's a wild animal. But from

With everything rationed during the whole of the 1940s, queues like this one, in Kent, were typical at shops. (War and Peace Archives)

what we saw of him he was very good, worse luck. So that's why Arsenal lost, the fog was so thick that they couldn't see either the ball or each other. But they were 2-0 up at half-time, so it looked as though everything was going okay. But in the second half, although Arsenal scored again, these Russians scored four goals to win the game 4-3. We heard afterwards that it was found that they had had twelve players on the field for at least twenty minutes of the second half, so that's another reason why they won. What a blooming swizz.

Reconstruction

King George VI makes a broadcast on the wireless: 'The time of destruction is over, the era of reconstruction begins.' I think he means that new houses are going to be built. Why don't grown-ups say things properly so that we can all understand them?

Rationing is still in place, which means no end to the queueing, and we haven't much in the way of food or clothes. Mums have to be registered at each shop they go to – grocer's, butcher's, fishmonger's and greengrocer's.

But there are some good things happening as well. One of these is a new serial on the wireless about a secret agent. Starting in October 1946, this goes out at

6.45 p.m. five nights a week and it's called *Dick Barton, Special Agent.* This is super and every kid in Britain is quickly riveted by it. Even girls are thrilled listening to the adventures of Dick and his sidekicks. Playing in the streets and woods stops at this time every night as we all rush home to listen to the next exciting instalment. Those lucky enough to have roller skates, now back in the shops, get home before the rest of us of course, the lucky sods.

One thing we don't really understand is the saying that times are hard, we must all make do and mend. This may be true, but no one has told us this piece of news. For boys and girls it's make your own toys and simply go out and do what kids do best, and that's have a really great time.

Two

HOME LIFE

Home in the 1940s is a mixture of comfort and fear. Nothing is as it should be because of the war with Germany. So the big disadvantage is that your house could be hit the next time German bombers come over.

Bath Night

By day, things are pretty much as they had always been. Well, mum is having trouble getting enough for us to eat, but in every other way life goes on. Bath night in particular is something none of us really look forward to because of all the trouble that it causes. Mum lights the gas under the copper that she uses every time she needs hot water. All of our washing is done in this as well. When the water is hot

An essential piece of kitchen equipment in 1940s houses, this is the copper. Note the stick on top used to poke the washing down, the tongs for getting it out, and the tap at the bottom to empty the water.

enough she turns on the tap at the bottom and fills up the small bowl. Then when this is full, she tips it into the bath. This has to be done quite a lot of times before there's enough water to wash in. The children in the house have to take it in turns to use the bath, with the 'ladies first' rule always used. It's bad enough having to wait your turn, but if you're a boy this means climbing into a bath full of lukewarm water that your sisters have just got out of, then having to sit crammed at one end of the tin bath while your brother does the same at the other. After a few minutes' playing time in comes mum and the washing starts. We're rubbed all over with hard Sunlight soap and when we have our hair washed as well; it's torture. 'Keep your eyes closed,' she says, as she rubs that soap across the top of our heads, and boy does that hurt. If you don't keep your eyes shut the soap gets into them and the pain is even worse.

Stepping out we're rubbed raw with a big towel before being allowed to put on clean underwear – vest and pants that are fully interlocking. None of us know what that means, only that the pants are sometimes longer than the short trousers that we wear and sometimes show beneath the legs of these. It makes us look daft and most of us hate these things.

Mealtimes

Mealtimes are always done in the same way, with the girls laying the table. When the food is ready all of the family sit up at it. Mum watches all her children to make sure they eat as much as they can, because waste in a time of war is certainly frowned upon. All leftover food is collected and used to feed pigs. The meat from these animals goes on sale to us, but only if you have enough coupons as well as the money to pay for it. That's provided the butcher your mum is registered at has any left by the time she gets to the head of the queue.

Once the meal is over, we have a filling pudding like spotted dick (suet pudding with currents in) with custard or rice pudding (both made with powdered milk), to make up for the fact that none of us had any meat in our dinner again. Mum has had to make do with a lot of gravy to make the meal look right. Permission has to be given for us to get down from the table. So the polite request is given, 'I've finished, can I get down please?'

Younger girls take care of putting meals into the oven to be kept warm for their older sisters who are out to work. In the later part of 1940 this means working in shops or factories making things like shoes or gloves. But from 1940 until the end of the war in 1945 they were doing much more dangerous work, such as filling bombs with gunpowder for our soldiers to shoot at the Germans. A lot of accidents happened and girls were killed as the explosives they were putting into the shell cases went off. Others were land girls who worked on farms, or they drove buses and ambulances, Princess Elizabeth even did this. Some flew Spitfires and delivered them to our boys at different airfields. Most older brothers have been called up to fight in the war.

Jobs for the Kids

All around the house, chores have to be done and kids are expected to do them. We've all helped with putting brown paper on to the windows to stop the glass shattering in an air raid. But other things need doing on a weekly basis as well. Washday brought the agony of mangle duty, and this was hard work.

First, though, the washing has to be done. This means the gas boiler in the kitchen being lit again. Into this mums put soda, then a washing powder, usually either Rinso or Oxadol. If there are things that are really dirty mums put these into the small bowl, then, using a washboard, they scrub the offending items until they look clean. When dads return home they need shirts washed in this way. Then the cuffs and collars, which they have to attach to the shirt with studs, are soaked in starch. Boy do we all thank our lucky stars the shirts we wear have collars attached. Okay, putting these shirts on isn't the easiest thing in the world to do – pulling them over your head before getting your arms into the sleeves, then pulling the whole thing down and tucking it in – but it's a blooming sight easier than struggling with starched collars and those awkward studs. Now, with the washing and rinsing done, it's mangle time, a chore all of us hate. Mangles are great big things with a wheel on top that brings the rollers closer together to squeeze more water out before the whole lot goes on the line. Mum stands on one side feeding the washing into the rollers. Sisters stand behind taking the washing out and putting it into a bowl. Turning the handle? Yes it's us, the kids. Trying to turn something that's almost as big as you are, with bulky washing going through the rollers, is nothing short of slave labour – sheer hard work that requires more than one boy. Usually two are on the wheel and at the end of the chore both are simply worn out with the effort they have had to put in to keep those rollers turning.

Then the ironing has to be done. Mum uses flat irons for this. They have to be heated up on the gas stove and when they're hot enough they're used to iron the sheets and clothes. One iron at a time is used while the other one is being heated up. Mum goes backwards and forwards to the scullery to change

Provisions for most families were kept in cupboards such as this. Note the McVitie & Price biscuit tin and the packet of Robin starch, along with other essentials.

irons so that she always has a hot one for use. Many a shirt has the burnt imprint of one of these irons left on it because it was too hot when she started using it. Instead of just getting the creases out of the material it was scorched black and there was nothing that could be done about it. Some homes have electric irons that have to be plugged into the light socket in the parlour, but most of our mums use the flat ones.

Money is so tight that a visit from the gas man – who comes to empty the meter – is very welcome. A lot of gas is used in the house, the cooker, copper and sometimes lights as well. The meters take a penny a time (1*d*) so when it is emptied the man puts the pennies into two piles. One of these goes into his collecting bag, but the other is given back to the lady of the house. This is called rebate. It's a funny word, but it means we get some money back to spend on the things we need.

Mums worked hard all day long to look after their families. Most houses have at least six children of varying ages all of whom have to be fed and clothed, and homes have to be kept clean and tidy. Lino is on the floors in all of the rooms and this has to be polished. A big tin of Ronuck floor polish is used for this.

Everywhere, homes needed to be ready when the siren sounds to let us know another air raid was starting. Most mums and grannies have all the documents a family needs in a bag that can be grabbed and taken to the shelter with the family. Babies sleep in the bottom drawer of their mother's sideboard. This is pulled out, with baby still inside, and also taken to the shelter. Some homes didn't do this. They had tables in the parlour made of strong steel. Anyone sitting underneath one of these has a very good chance of surviving a direct hit on their house. They were called Morrison shelters, or to give them their proper name, Table (Morrison) Indoor Shelters. They were designed by a man named John Baker and named after the Minister of Home Security, Herbert Morrison. Under the stairs is another popular place to sit for protection, but if a bomb did land on the house these people had to be dug out of the rubble afterwards.

Through war and peace, most houses have a lot in common: tin baths and outside toilets, which you have to leave the warmth of your bed and venture outside to in the dark. It's not easy, even in the summer. Spiders like to lurk there and finding one, especially at night, makes even boys rush back into the house as soon as they can. In winter this operation is simply horrible as the cold is unbearable. Sometimes when you pull the chain afterwards nothing happens because the water in the cistern has frozen. Telling mum about this she yells back, 'Alright, leave it. I'll put some water down tomorrow.' This is the only way to free the toilet when the chain is out of operation – buckets of water poured down the toilet pan until only clean water is left.

Bedrooms at this time of year are not the best places to be, either. It's so cold that the windows freeze over, and not only outside. The inside has a layer of ice, and the room is absolutely freezing as a result. Children in most houses are allowed to have an overcoat on top of the sheet and two brown blankets to cover them. Stories of rivalry are common.

A small boy sleeping next to his older brother woke to find the overcoat being dragged from his bed. The smaller boy of course put up a fight, with the result being the arm of the overcoat getting pulled off. Rushing downstairs, he burst in on his mother.

'Mum, David has pulled the sleeve off the overcoat on my bed.'

His mother was entertaining one of her neighbours. Wanting to keep her reputation as a fairly well-off lady intact, she quickly corrected her youngest son.

'It's not an overcoat Johnnie, it's an eiderdown.'

'Oh, sorry. David has pulled the sleeve off of the eiderdown on my bed.'

In the morning there's a race downstairs to the parlour where mum has a nice fire burning in the kitchen range. We can get dressed in the warmth from this. These small ranges have an oven beside a small enclosure where the fire is burning. Mums can use this for baking bread and things like that. The range itself has to be cleaned out each morning and last night's ashes taken out to the dustbin. Black lead makes the kitchen range look like new. When it's gleaming and the fire inside is burning brightly it's so welcoming on these freezing mornings. Then wash and clean your teeth out in the scullery, before sitting down to breakfast before the trek to school. Breakfast is often bread and dripping, with arguments over who gets most of the meat essence that sinks to the bottom of the bowl where the dripping is kept.

At night bread is toasted using the home-made fork that either dad or granddad has made. This is wire twisted together with the ends pulled out and formed into forks. This pierces the bread and then it is held right up against the bars that all kitchen ranges have, where the heat is greatest. The result is toast that tastes absolutely marvellous. Okay, it's a bit burnt but that helps it taste even better, and spread with either margarine or dripping it's such a great way to end any day.

Boys and girls help mums around the house – the girls help with washing and cooking as well as bed-making and some housework, while boys do the physical jobs. Along with mangle duty, there is always something that needs mending and of course the gardening has to be done as well. Most dads, before they went off to war, taught their sons the art of mending shoes. This is done in the garden shed or scullery with a home-made shoehorn. The leather is cut to size then fitted and nailed on. With leather being in such short supply now, make do and mend is put into practice. Strong cardboard is used for soling and heeling, but in very poor homes holes are filled by placing thick newspaper inside the shoe. This keeps the feet of children away from the hard road surfaces and lasts a few days until the paper shreds and new a lot is put in. Newspaper is also used as toilet paper. This is cut into small squares and stuck on a hook behind the outside toilet door.

The garden was very important, both during and after the war. Vegetables are still being grown to help feed large families, and chickens, rabbits, and in some cases pigs, are kept to help with the feeding. Supplies of coal, bread, milk, and sometimes vegetables, are brought door-to-door by a man with a horse and cart. The coal is humped on to the backs of these big, strong men, who carry it through the house and dump it into the coal bin outside. These men didn't go away to fight during the war because they have what our mums say are reserved occupations. We suppose that makes sense, because that coal is heavy and it takes strong men to carry it. They bring a hundredweight at a time, and this has to be used very sparingly. It costs a lot of money so mums are careful how much is burnt every day. And guess who has to go out in all weathers to get some more of this fuel, using the brass coal scuttle? Yes of course, it's us children, girls as well as boys. The horses have their uses too, of course. For one thing they are a means of fertilising the garden. Their manure is great for potatoes and all other root vegetables, and the rhubarb grows so well when this natural source of fertiliser is spread. Children follow the horses wherever they go. Once a horse raises its tail, this means get ready to swoop. The horse is about to answer the call of nature and the boys are waiting to say thank you very much as they rush to shovel the result of this into the buckets they carry. Some of this goes on to their gardens, but a lot is sold to neighbours. Money is so tight that pocket money is out of the question, so this is a means of getting a few pennies to buy sweets and other things.

Watering the garden happens in the evenings, if it isn't raining of course. Not many homes have anything as luxurious as a watering can, so dad or granddad had got over this awkward situation by keeping an empty baked bean tin. Instead of going into the dustbin, it's washed out and holes are punched into the bottom. Then with a full bucket of water we hardy gardeners go to work, dipping the tin in to fill it up, then bringing it out and swishing it backwards and forwards over our vegetables. The water runs out through the holes in the bottom and the effect is the same as if it were coming out of the spout of a watering can.

The Importance of the Cabbage Patch

Cabbages are very important and most gardens have a patch. They're important not only for our dinners, but because this is where big birds called storks bring babies when mums want another one for their families. They fly with a cloth in their beaks where the new baby is kept until the stork leaves it in the cabbage patch in your back garden. Not many are being delivered while the war is on though because, as mums keep telling us, those rotten Germans are shooting the storks down so they won't be able to bring any babies.

The NHS

It was after the war too that something called The National Health Service started, in 1948 under the Health Secretary, Aneurin Bevin. We don't know what this means but our mums are very happy about it. A man from the Houses of Parliament had started it and we can get free healthcare. It means mums don't have to pay the doctor if any of us get ill and they can't treat us themselves.

When I'm Cleaning Windows

It's not easy to say which of our chores, whether cooking, cleaning or shopping, is the most boring as far as boys are concerned. Cleaning, for instance, means we have to do the outside of windows, and boy is this hard work. We have to wash the glass with hot water and Sunlight soap, then rinse them off and make sure we don't leave any smears. The insides are done by the girls, which up until 1945 wasn't at all easy because of all the brown tape. After the war it didn't get any easier. Once the soapy water is off the glass it has to be polished, and this is done with newspaper. Rolled up into balls it has to be applied to the glass and rubbed until the windows shine. This is hard enough, but with your granny sitting inside the window, watching you all the time, it isn't funny at all. Her glare can be felt as you rub that newspaper over it, then, when your arms are aching from the effort, she will rap the glass and point to a part that you have missed. Why do they have such eagle eyes? This is really hard work and not something that Britain's adventurous boys should be doing.

Inside, most houses look the same. The kitchen, which some call the scullery, is at the back, downstairs. This has a sink, a gas cooker, gas copper and places where mums can get food ready, chopping vegetables, rolling out pastry and stuff. A small bowl is also kept here and used for washing and filling the tin bath. The cats' dishes are here as well. We have them to keep the mice down.

The parlour has two armchairs, one on each side of the kitchen range; a settee; a table in the middle where we all eat our meals; and mum's sideboard. This has drawers where knives and forks are kept and cupboards for tins of food and stuff like that. The cups and saucers and all of her plates are kept here too. Our entertainment comes from the wireless that sits on top.

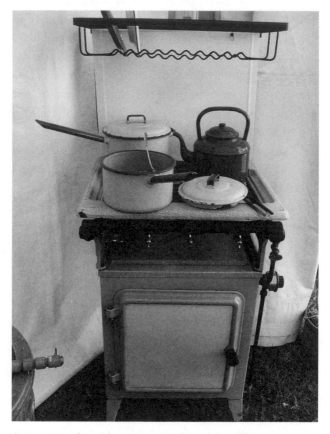

A 1940s gas cooker – I have memories of my own mother using one just like this. All of the cooking pots are made of enamel.

A cabinet found in the parlour, with cups and saucers on view. Also visible is the Bakelite radio we all called the wireless.

In some homes mums have what's called a Welsh dresser. This is a great big thing with plates stacked on to shelves along with side plates and saucers, while the teacups are hung on hooks. These also have cupboards for tinned stuff and anything else that won't go off. And we all have a bread bin where loaves, wrapped in tissue paper, are kept.

The meat safe that was found in so many houses during this decade. These were the forerunners of the refrigerator. (War and Peace Archives)

Upstairs is one big bedroom. Mums and sisters sleep in this room, and if gran and granddad live in the house as well they have the room next to this. This leaves the boys sharing the only bedroom left, and that's the small one at the back. This is so small that often only one bed can fit into it, so they have to share. Two can sleep at the top of this in the normal way. But if the family has three or more boys, it's two at one end and the rest at the bottom.

It's comfortable enough, and most kids live this way, so no one ever feels they are worse off than anyone else. The floors are all covered with lino, upstairs and down, and this is cold to walk on in the winter. Still, it's better that bare floorboards. Whatever any of us thinks of these houses, they are where we live so we love every part of them. Long live our country and our homes.

Three

STREETS: PLAYING ON AND BOMB DAMAGE

The war dominates 1940 but that doesn't stop boys and girls everywhere from playing their games in the streets and generally having a great time. Outside every morning, when you get home from the shelters, roads are covered with rubble. In some cases no houses are left intact. This makes playing marbles (allies) hard to do because this is played in the gutters. If they're filled with bricks and stuff you can't roll your allies along can you? The school playground is the place to do this now, as well as conkers when the right time of year comes around. But the streets still hold a lot of attention for children, and all of us take full advantage of the bomb damage.

Houses in places like London, Manchester, Liverpool and big towns and cities like these have cellars, and when one can be found in a bombed-out ruin it makes a brilliant hideout. Boys can make their own headquarters and woe betide any from the other roads coming round and trying to take them over. The camps are set up as soon as the civil defence blokes have finished digging people out of the ruins and saying the house, shop or office building is now clear. That means no one is supposed to go inside because the buildings aren't safe.

Try telling that to British boys. We're not called British bulldog for nothing. In no time at all a cellar can become not only your gang's headquarters but also the headquarters of your spy set-up. We're fighting the Germans as well. In our games, though, we always win every battle.

Every one of us has his own tin helmet, usually an old saucepan that didn't disappear with the rest of the stuff for the war effort. They work well enough but the handle that sticks out behind your head is a bit of a nuisance. The girls sometimes join in and they become nurses. Boys then have to put up with bandages tied round their heads, legs and arms. It's okay really, because the girls have learned first aid at school and even practised it on their dolls. But when they start trying to throw out the old clothes we keep because they're torn and dirty, arguments soon break out.

Most of us have our favourite clothes that we play in all the time and we keep a lot of them in our camps. We change into different ones for whatever game we're playing. So what if they are dirty? We're soldiers so we can't be expected to be clean as well, can we? Girls will never understand this.

They make do the same as us, and they are already finding old pushchairs and prams from houses that have been bombed. These are used for their dollies and they push them around the streets looking just like their mums. It's funny when you see them helping with the family shopping, the grown-up with her undamaged pram with a real baby in it, and her daughter with her rescued pram with a doll.

Some of us have roller skates and even play football wearing them. You have to be good at this before you can hope to get a game though. Leapfrog is another favourite. The annoying thing here is that the girls sometimes join in and are just as good at it as we are. It's played in the streets as well as playgrounds and is not just one boy leaping over the back of another. It's played with a least six boys bending over in a line, then the same number take a run and leap on to their backs. At least six usually manage this feat, though the boy at the end only just gets there and has to hang on very tightly indeed to stop himself from falling off.

Some roads have big shelters, so playing in these is not so easy. With rubble from houses that have been hit as well, there's not much chance for chasing games. A lot of shrapnel lands on these shelters, though, so the morning after a raid, much to the annoyance of the civil defence blokes, hordes of boys can be found on the roofs eagerly snatching these war souvenirs. Skipping (girls), dibs (boys and girls), marbles (boys) and war games (boys and girls) keep us going all through the dark days of war

Scrumping

What of the kids who have been evacuated? They go to lovely country schools and do dancing and swimming and stuff. The boys from the big cities are amazed at the opportunities for apple scrumping. The country children aren't very pleased when these boys from big towns come into their midst, go to their schools and play in their fields and woods. But they know it has to be accepted because of the danger faced all the time in these places. Most manage to adapt alright, but at scrumping time they are not prepared to give up their right to the orchards in their villages. Town boys, of course, are streetwise from a very early age. They have to be to survive all the time. So they quickly set up their own scrumping pitches and many a fight starts up when the country boys find out about it. Britain may be at war with Germany, but once the apples are ready for picking the war takes another turn altogether. It's town against country, as apples are plucked from the trees and into the pockets of short trousers.

The bomb damage is everywhere because of the nightly raids. Even one Underground station has been destroyed by a direct hit in London (Balham, 14 October 1940). A lot of people, grown-ups as well as children, were killed down there, and that's not funny at all. The next day a double-decker bus fell into the great hole in the road, but the driver and conductor got out and were alright.

Coventry has been left a shell of how it was before. All the factories that produced cars are now turning out things needed by our soldiers, so the Germans have tried to stop this by wiping the whole city out. In the South of England they have targeted Portsmouth, because of its naval dockyard, Plymouth for the same reason and Southampton for the docks and spitfire assembly. Then up through the country, anywhere where large towns and cities stood, the bombs rained down: Liverpool, Bolton, Manchester, Leeds, Middlesbrough. In Wales, Cardiff and Swansea were hit, and not forgetting Scotland whose shipyards in places like the Clyde were also attacked. That bloke Hitler really wants to destroy all of our homes and bring our great nation to its knees. Who is he kidding? Our Prime Minister as well as our wonderful

King George VI go into these places, talking to the people who live there. They are a rallying call for the British people to stand firm; we will win the war and stop the Germans in their tracks.

Another problem is what our mothers call 'looting'. This means crooks going into a freshly bombed house and stealing anything they can find that is worth money. This is a dirty trick and the police are always on the lookout for these people. Families of course can go back to what's left of their homes to try and salvage anything they can. Once this has been done whatever is left in the ruins is fair game. We children take full advantage of that and acquire a lot of things we can use in our camps.

One interesting thing happened to a boy in our neighbourhood and it concerned his bike. His home had been bombed and he and his family moved in with relatives. Once that was done his dad went to the ruins to get what he could. When he got back he told his son that the bike was still there; although the house was a complete wreck, somehow the bike had survived and was still usable. 'We'll go back tomorrow and get it son,' he said, but when father and son did return the next day the bike had gone. Someone had seen it and taken it for themself. Just a few days later this same boy was summoned to his headmaster's study. Not a good thing for any boy to hear, usually this meant he was in trouble. On entering he saw his best friend stood in front of the headmaster's desk and, amazingly, his bike, leaning against the wall. He was asked to identify it as his and when he did, was told his friend had been caught riding it and was now going to be punished for stealing. He watched him receive six of the best from the headmaster's cane. Although he was very pleased to get the bike back, he felt guilty that his friend had been punished for doing what he and the rest of them would have done in the same situation. A bike found in the ruins of a house was a prize indeed. Any boy would have quickly grabbed this and claimed it for their own.

The End of the War

In May 1945 it's all over. There are big headlines in the papers on 2 May telling us that Hitler is dead. He died fighting to the end, it says, but grown-ups know he took his own life and good riddance they're saying. He appointed Grand Admiral Karl Doenitz to take over, so this navy officer is now the new German 'fewerer' (fuehrer). We can never get that word right. This is the man who used German U-boats against us, and our sailors called him Admiral Donuts. But he was good at his job, as we are being told all the time.

Children enjoy a treat the like of which none of us have ever experienced, a party in our own road.

VE DAY + 4

The war is over and this is one of many parties given for children in celebration of this. This one shows the VE Day party in Belgrave Road, Southampton. (The Ford family)

Mums all over the country have pulled together and used their coupons to get cakes, biscuits, jelly and custard and all sorts of things to put into sandwiches. The younger ones especially have never eaten or even seen some of these things before. For them, even more than us, this is a miracle. We've won the war and Hitler is gone. Big headlines fill the newspapers and a celebration is going on all over Britain. No more will

German planes nvade our country and try to destroy our buildings.

The shelters in the roads are quickly taken away. Great big cranes arrive, with a huge ball on the end of a chain swinging through the air and crashing into the bricks, sending them flying in all directions. Every time it lands we cheer. Empty roads means allies (marbles) can be played properly as well as Dinky toys that are now being made again. Only war toys like tanks, battleships and warplanes were produced while the war was on. Model cars, with wheels freshly oiled to make them go faster and further, are being sent racing down the gutters. The girls get in the way sometimes with their long skipping ropes, but we have to put up with that.

Street lighting is back on now. A man comes round in the evening on a bike with a long pole that has a hook on the end. He rides up to all the lamp posts in the road, and skilfully hooks the lever at the top of the lamp post and gives it a jerk. This turns the light on, so he now moves on to the next one and does the same thing until all the lights in the road are on. In the mornings he comes round and turns them all off again. We watch this every time it happens and will him to miss, so that he has to ride round again. This doesn't happen very often because these blokes are good at doing it, but when it does how they must hate us as we hoot with laughter at them.

Anyway we're all experts at turning the street lights on and off. Alright, we weren't allowed to do it during the war because all the roads had to be blacked out. But now we can get back to what we were doing before it started – climbing the lamp posts and working the switch at the top ourselves. While the war is on a lot of us use these posts as anchors for our ropes. These are tied around the top, our climbing experience coming in handy for this. Then groups of us use the ropes to swing round and round, and boy is that fun. The only thing we need to be careful about is when they are painted. A sign saying 'wet paint' is always left to warn people to avoid a newly painted lamp post, but boys being boys, these are often removed to make our rivals have to go home and explain to their mothers how the front of their clothes as well as large parts of their bare legs are now covered in green paint. Many a bottom stings for a long time after this happens. In some places gas lighting is still used in the streets and roads. Men have to come round with a ladder that they climb in order to light the gas in the evenings, and then of course they come round in the morning to turn them all off again.

Children that were born at the start of 1940 should be streetwise by now. Normally this would happen naturally. Small children would watch their older brothers and sisters and in this way learn all about the neighbourhood where they lived. But while the war still raged and sirens were going off all the time, mothers had to know where their children were. They knew that the older ones would be kept as safe as possible in the shelters at their schools, but the young ones who were at home needed to be kept close at all times. In the shelters these young boys and girls sat huddled as close to their mothers as possible while outside the world was going mad. They had no understanding of fear, so the falling of the bombs didn't affect them as it did the grown-ups.

Now, though, with peace once more being enjoyed, the young ones have a lot of catching up to do. They don't know their way around or any of the main playgrounds, woods or rivers. It means older boys especially having to take their younger brothers around with them until they can join with other kids of their own age and go it alone. It's a big nuisance and your mates aren't exactly happy either. After all, you don't want the job of having to watch over a little kid when you're at the river, swinging out over the water on a rope that's tied to a tree. You simply want to enjoy the experience, and maybe the added problem of the rope slipping out of your hands so that you fall into the water. Your clothes get soaking wet and mothers aren't going to be pleased when you get home, but that's what playing is all about. It's fun as well as dodgy at times. Everyone goes into the water at one time or another, and sometimes into thick mud as well. But with younger brothers along all you can do is watch your mates having a great time while you keep a stern eye on the kid. But at least we both have a good laugh at the boys who do fall in the water.

Roads that are clear of shelters have the added opportunity of fun games, such as knock the door and run away. Why do the grown-ups get so angry about that? It's nowhere near the fright they've experienced for so long. But children everywhere are getting back to simply being children again, so this game has been reintroduced.

Road Repairs

Roads are the first to be repaired. Many have either taken a direct hit or had damage caused by the blast of bombs falling close to them. The men who have come back to their jobs with the council are now out repairing road surfaces. This is a fascination for both boys and girls, though all of us shy away from the noise of the pneumatic drills. When the big steam-rollers come along and go backwards and forwards over the tar that has been put down to flatten it, kids everywhere run along beside them and watch the man driving, turning the handles and putting coal in the firebox. They make a noise but they're smashing things to watch. Never get in the way of one of these, though, as the huge roller in the front would very soon squash a kid.

Some houses that survive the bombing have problems for years after. Many a story is told of things happening inside them, and one in particular stands out. A man had just come home from work and his wife put his dinner on the table, the children of the house having eaten theirs earlier. So he sat alone, as so many other dads did then. Before he could start eating, though, there was an ominous noise above his head. Without any warning the ceiling in the room collapsed down on top of him. He wasn't hurt by this but his dinner was ruined. After inspection the man and his wife were told this had happened because of all the bombing in the area during the war. This house wasn't hit, but a lot in the area were. It was the blast of those bombs that shook all the other buildings around them and a lot suffered structural damage as a result. This is why the ceiling collapsed.

Boys Will Be Boys

Boys everywhere take full advantage of these bombed houses with camps in the cellars underneath. If you are lucky enough to find a bombed house that still had a banister intact you're in heaven. Mothers never let us slide down ours at home, and schoolteachers would have a fit if you tried it there. But in a bombed-out ruin no one is around to say no when you climb on the banister. There is the odd accident as sometimes more than one boy at a time climbs on and we all slide down together. This puts more of a strain on the already weakened shell of the house. More than once it leads to the whole banister coming away from the wall, dumping the boys on to the floor. This often gives way as well, so the boys concerned land back in the cellar with cuts and bruises and ruined clothes. The one threat we all look out for is the appearance of a policeman. We aren't supposed to play in these ruins because of the danger of collapse, so a sentry has to be posted at all times when we are inside. If any of us are caught inside a bombed-out house justice is dished out in the form of a clout round the ear from the copper's rolled up leather gloves, and boy does that hurt.

Girls join the boys in these cellar camps and come with us as we hunt in the ruins for the things we need for playing. Bike wheels that are still intact are prime targets. Once you find a frame, a bike can be put together and ridden up and down the roads. Okay they don't have anything as luxurious as tyres and pedals, but you can't have everything, can you? Brakes are also missing, but with the skilful use of feet they can be stopped if really necessary. Putting these bikes into any form so that they could be ridden is a job for a grown-up, and this is where these new dads that had come so suddenly into our lives come in handy. They know about these things and can tighten nuts much better than any of us.

Girls are champions at skipping, as we boys have to admit, but another thing they do is handstands. They rush at a wall then plant their hands down on the pavement and kick their legs into the air until their feet come to rest on the wall above their heads. Some of us can do handstands but the girls are more elegant when they do them. Or most of them are anyway, those that tuck their skirts or dresses into the bottom legs of their underwear before doing the handstand. But if they don't, or if their clothes come out of their underwear, they find their dresses or skirts coming down over their heads. We, of course, being young gentlemen, look the other way when this happens, so as not to embarrass the girls. None of us ever have a sneak peek – though if anyone believes this then they'll believe anything!

The girls keep up their search for old prams they could use for their dolls, but very soon they come into conflict with us as we find a new use for the wheels. Boys start building – with dads' help again – soapbox trolleys: a board with a box on the back to act as a seat, two wheels in front and two at the back, and there it was. Every boy's dream, they hurtle down slopes with one and sometimes two at a time on board. Races are organised and girls take part, acting as starters and also standing at the end of a run to flag the winner over the finish line. Many accidents happen and small injuries are sustained as well as damage to clothing. But that's what playing is all about and no one, not even a bloke by the name of Adolf Hitler, can stop British children from doing it.

Four

GAMES, HOBBIES AND PASTIMES

Hoops are one of the things we all like playing with and they are quite easy to obtain. Children before us had these from shops and were ready to play with them straight away. In this time of so many shortages, however, we have to fend for ourselves. Mums have to be careful with money. Certainly this can't be used on something like a hoop, or any other toy, except on our birthdays, when mums perform miracles and give us a party with our friends.

On the table are things that make our eyes come out on stalks. Sandwiches, cakes, jelly and ice cream, wow. Then and only then, except for Christmas, do we have toys that are bought from a shop, and these are things like models of planes or ships that have to be built using the glue from the box. Girls get dollies and some of these were super as they shut their eyes and cry when they are tipped up. They also get things like dainty handkerchiefs and ribbons for their hair.

Outside in the roads, though, things like hoops are home-made. They are quite simply old bicycle wheels that can be found all over the place in bombed-out ruins. Once dad or granddad has used his pliers to take out all the spokes we are left with the outer rim of the wheel and they make super hoops. With a stick in your hand they are propelled along the pavements at speed, bowled along by being repeatedly hit with the stick and guided with this as well. Brushing the inside rim of the hoop turns it to the left, and the outside turns it to the right. Boys and even girls become masters of these and races soon become popular. A set course is marked out with someone stationed along it to make sure no rule-breaking is going on (taking shortcuts is not uncommon). Then at the word 'Go!' the participants send their hoops into motion and the race is on. This worked better after the war was over and the roads were cleared of rubble.

Played with in the roads as well as indoors are spinning tops. Popular with both boys and girls, they can be made to spin very fast indeed and contests are soon going on to see whose could go on spinning the longest. The large tops are sent spinning by a thin cord being wrapped around it. With a big pull this is released and this action starts the top spinning. There are also small versions of these where the string is wrapped around in a groove. Then, mostly boys, swing the end of the string so that it is let out in an action similar to that of a whip and the small tops are sent both spinning and at the same time flying through the air. Competitions are soon started here as well to see who can throw these the furthest while still spinning.

As so many men come round delivering things using horses and carts, it is great fun to pinch a ride as they come down your street. All of us join in together and hang on to the back of the cart. It is super, that is until the man driving the horse hears us laughing and not only shouts at us to clear off but waves his whip as well. We aren't really cheeky but as we ran away some of us make gestures to the man. This is putting your thumb up against your nose while wiggling the rest of your fingers at him. We all think this is funny but grown-ups get mad and say we should respect our elders, and not make such rude gestures towards them.

Indoors on wet days and in the evenings, families, especially after the war when dads are home again, listen to the wireless and also play games we can all join in with. Favourites among them are snakes and ladders, ludo, draughts (granddads are best at this and we can never win when we played against them), and some card games. Snap is a good game for us to play. All you need to win is a sharp eye and loud voice to shout when two cards of different suits land on the pile in the middle with the same number or picture on them. Another game with cards is happy families, where you have to guess who has the right people in their hand to complete a family in yours.

Wooden toys and in some cases rag dolls amuse the girls, but they have to watch out, because if a boy gets hold of one of these he will always be very reluctant to give it back to his sister. They make absolutely smashing dolls to be shot or killed with a spear and then placed on the top stair so they roll over and over until they reach the bottom of the staircase. This rolling movement looks just like a real dead body rolling down, and they always finish up crumpled on the floor. Perfect. Boys keep this up for as long as the doll lasts before, full of 'spear holes' – from needles – it falls to pieces.

Hobbies

A lot of kids like collecting things and some have very good collections as a result. Shrapnel is one, but also stamps are collected and stuck into albums. While the war is on not many letters arrive, and hardly any with foreign stamps on them. But kids with relations who had gone to other countries to live wait with bated breath for them to write home. When a letter drops through the box, posted from another country, mum keeps the envelope so that when her sons come home from school it is presented to the one whose turn it is to have the stamp. This turn-and-turn-about method stops arguments breaking out among boys who think they are losing out.

Cigarette cards have also been in short supply, but after the war they start arriving again. Boys wait until their dads run out of cigarettes and buy more from their local tobacconist. Then it is time to queue up to get your share of the cards inside the packets. They feature sportsmen and some film stars as well, and having a large collection is something to be proud of. The way to get a big collection is to be good at flicking these. Contests with other boys take place. The cards are lined up against a wall and the object is to knock as many down with your flicked card as possible. The ones you knock down you keep.

A keen eye is needed by those boys whose hobby is collecting either cigarette packets or matchboxes. These treasured things can sometimes be found as you walk the gutters. So many smokers, mostly men, simply throw away an empty cigarette packet or matchbox before going to the shop to buy some more. Finding them in this way means you can increase your collection at no cost at all. They are usually kept in a shoebox at home, and many a boy swaps these with his school friends.

A lot of boys have super collections of marbles and some have special bags their mums have made for them to keep these in. Conkers are kept year by year to give us all the chance to get them hardened for the conker season when that comes round after the summer holidays. There are simple ways of doing this and many a lad knows them. First put a hole through your conkers with a meat skewer, if your mum has got one. Then soak them in vinegar overnight (begging your mum for this if she hasn't got much in the larder for all of the family's food). Then in the morning, with mum's permission and help, they go into the oven and are baked hard. What a great chance you then have of winning lots of conker fights and one of your conkers ending up as a twenty-oner, the envy of any playground.

Many a boy notes down car and railway steam engine numbers, and some even collect bus tickets. These have a number across the top, and to get one where these numbers added up to twenty-one – the coming-of-age year – was a prize indeed. Boys offered these to girls they liked and the girls were thrilled to have something that was the envy of the playground presented to them.

Fun at the seaside after the war. These children are all in the bathing costumes of the time. The girls have costumes of the same material, while most of the boys are wearing trunks. Just one lad has the over the shoulder costume that boys still wore. (War and Peace Archives)

Mums make quite a fuss when you get home because your clothes haven't dried and you're sent to bed as a punishment, but for us this is simply fun and we all go on doing it despite the punishments dished out to us.

Home-made Bikes

Riding our home-made bikes is fun as well, although it's better to find land where a bombed-out build-ing once stood because of the opportunities for races

Pastimes

Most kids, boys and girls, like nothing more than playing in the streets and bombsites across Great Britain. But there are other things to do as well, one of which is swimming in lakes and rivers. Girls wear proper swimming costumes, which cover all of their bodies except their arms and legs, but boys go into the water in a variety of swimwear. Some have trunks that cover just the lower part of their bodies, others the bathing costumes that go up over their shoulders so their chests are covered as well. But mainly, with town kids, swimming is done while fully clothed or stripped down to underwear. After all, this is so much better than having to wear swimming costumes that your mum or granny has knitted for you. These woollen costumes look alright when you first put them on and they're dry, but once you've been in the water they droop alarmingly when you come out. Other boys, and embarrassingly girls as well, laugh and point at you as you drag yourself away and hurriedly get changed back into your clothes.

To make this more exciting, ropes are tied to tree branches so that you can launch yourself into the air while hanging. This is high on the list of exciting and daring games. With the encouraging shouts from the bank to go higher, then shouts of 'let go' ringing in your ears, you drop straight down into the water.

One thing theirs doesn't have, though, is a crossbar. Boys' bikes have this and it makes us feel important that we have something that made us stand out from the girls. But sometimes lads slip while riding and come down hard on this crossbar, landing with one leg on either side of it. The result here is the boy lying on the ground with his legs drawn up under his tummy and crying with the pain. No one laughs at this because we all knew how awful it is.

Sheets of rusting corrugated tin can be found all over the place and we use them a lot. They're good for making camps among the ruined houses, and can also be used for sliding down steep banks. The trick here is to hold the sides of the sheet of tin you're sitting on and lean either to your right or left when making a turn. Gripping the sides of the tin and pulling it upwards as you lean means the turn is completed and you then go on to the end of the run. Simple, and a lot of fun, but why so many lads end up crashing and getting in a state with torn clothes and filthy arms and legs because they didn't make the turns was a mystery to the ones who were so good at it.

Home-made toys and bikes, shrapnel and other collections as well as the joy of swimming and riding fast on those ramshackle bikes makes the fun we all enjoy, not even the Germans could do anything about that.

꠸

and contests of skill. The other consideration is that grown-ups don't like the noise we make when riding on the pavements – well, without tyres they do clatter a lot. And without pedals either, it needs two boys, one each side, pushing as hard as they can to get you going. But anywhere you can find places with hills or even humps in the ground, these bikes go down without anyone having to push, and the speeds they travel at is so thrilling. However, because of the slight problem of the lack of brakes, if anything does go wrong while hurtling down a bank then there isn't a lot that can be done about it. Many a lad found this out to their cost as they rushed out of control and ended their run in some very awkward places. Crashing into someone's garden, straight through a fence, and even sometimes whizzing out of control and landing in a river, lake or stream. But we're boys and these disasters are laughed off – by us anyway. The grown-ups again shout at us for the damage to their gardens, and even dish out clips round the ear if we're not fast enough running away.

Girls never rode on these makeshift bikes, but a lot of them had ones that were nicknamed SPBs. This stood for spare parts bike, and they were made up in a lot of garden sheds by granddads or fathers if they were at home. The end product put ours to shame. They rode elegantly along on bikes with tyres, pedals, chains and of course the all-important brakes.

had gone to other countries to live wait with bated breath for them to write home. When a letter drops through the box, posted from another country, mum keeps the envelope so that when her sons come home from school it is presented to the one whose turn it is to have the stamp. This turn-and-turn-about method stops arguments breaking out among boys who think they are losing out.

Cigarette cards have also been in short supply, but after the war they start arriving again. Boys wait until their dads run out of cigarettes and buy more from their local tobacconist. Then it is time to queue up to get your share of the cards inside the packets. They feature sportsmen and some film stars as well, and having a large collection is something to be proud of. The way to get a big collection is to be good at flicking these. Contests with other boys take place. The cards are lined up against a wall and the object is to knock as many down with your flicked card as possible. The ones you knock down you keep.

A keen eye is needed by those boys whose hobby is collecting either cigarette packets or matchboxes. These treasured things can sometimes be found as you walk the gutters. So many smokers, mostly men, simply throw away an empty cigarette packet or matchbox before going to the shop to buy some more. Finding them in this way means you can increase your collection at no cost at all. They are usually kept in a shoebox at home, and many a boy swaps these with his school friends.

A lot of boys have super collections of marbles and some have special bags their mums have made for them to keep these in. Conkers are kept year by year to give us all the chance to get them hardened for the conker season when that comes round after the summer holidays. There are simple ways of doing this and many a lad knows them. First put a hole through your conkers with a meat skewer, if your mum has got one. Then soak them in vinegar overnight (begging your mum for this if she hasn't got much in the larder for all of the family's food). Then in the morning, with mum's permission and help, they go into the oven and are baked hard. What a great chance you then have of winning lots of conker fights and one of your conkers ending up as a twenty-oner, the envy of any playground.

Many a boy notes down car and railway steam engine numbers, and some even collect bus tickets. These have a number across the top, and to get one where these numbers added up to twenty-one – the coming-of-age year – was a prize indeed. Boys offered these to girls they liked and the girls were thrilled to have something that was the envy of the playground presented to them.

Five

ENTERTAINMENT, RADIO, MUSIC AND CLOTHES

Going to the pictures is something we enjoy, though while the war was on the picture houses as well as live theatres all start their programmes a lot earlier. It is so they end before eight o'clock in the evening. This is the time that most air raids started, so it isn't a good idea for a lot of people to be in the same building in case one of those German bombs hit it. If a raid does start before the picture ends or the stage show finishes, the manager of the theatre or picture house comes out on to the stage to let everyone know and give them the chance to leave and get into an air-raid shelter.

Stars like Vera Lynn go on entertaining on stage all through the war and give so much pleasure to every-one. She sings songs our mothers say are inspirational, and though we haven't a clue what that means, even we understand the sentiment of songs like 'We'll Meet Again' and 'There'll be Bluebirds over the White Cliffs of Dover'. She is a lovely lady and we all love listening to her on the wireless as much as our mothers and older sisters do.

We laugh at the comedies starring Arthur Askey (1900–82) and Richard Murdoch (1907–90), such the film *Bandwagon* (1940). This is the film of their show on the wireless, which we all enjoy listening to. To be able to go to the pictures and see them on the screen is really something.

Another big star who makes us laugh – even though we never know if the film we are watching will be interrupted by another flipping air raid – is Will Hay (1888–1949). We love the one he made in 1937, *Oh Mr Porter*. This is shown a lot because it is so popular. We all love trains, and this film, about a stationmaster (Will Hay) getting a job in an out-of-the-way station in Ireland, is hilarious. Another train picture comes out in 1940 and is just as good. It is called *The Ghost Train* and it stars Arthur Askey and Richard Murdoch. In 1941, Will Hay makes another ghost film, *The Ghost of St Michael's*. Boys and girls everywhere love these films because they're so funny. We can laugh ourselves silly watching them and forget, for a while anyway, all of the trouble that's going on outside.

George Formby (1904–61) is a Lancashire comedian and brilliant ukulele player and his film *Let George Do It* (1940) has us laughing our heads off. In this film he punches Mr Hitler on the nose and calls him a windbag. His other film that we like is called *Bell-Bottom George* (1943) and this makes us laugh as well. His ukulele playing in both films is super. Even on the wireless he got us all laughing and singing along with songs such as 'My Granddad's Flannelette Nightshirt', 'Auntie Maggie's Remedy', and 'Mr Wu's an Air-Raid Warden Now'. Many of us listening to him playing want to be just like him when we grow up.

And of course it isn't just us kids who find the films, some silent, of Stan Laurel (1890–1965) and Oliver Hardy (1892–1957) hilariously funny. Grownups everywhere laugh out loud when these two men are on the screen. They get into so many ridiculous situations and we just laugh ourselves out watching them. This is one reason why we all get through the war – none of us, even the youngest, ever forgets how to laugh.

We also love films with Old Mother Riley in them; she is just like so many of our grannies. She was played by someone called Arthur Lucan (1885–1954) – a funny name for a lady – and her daughter was called Kitty McShane (1897–1964). All of us know someone who looks just like Old Mother Riley, and we play games, with girls dressing up as this old washerwoman. The first picture we see is *Old Mother Riley Joins Up* (1939). Then throughout the rest of 1940 she makes more pictures and we love every one of them.

There is also a treat for us in 1940, when a picture about our favourite boy, *Just William*, comes out. We all love the books about this boy and his gang, because William is just like us. But the person who writes them is a lady called Richmal Crompton (1890–1969). We all ask ourselves what a lady can possibly know about boys and how we live and play. Oh well, I suppose we'll never know the answer to that, but the 'Just William' books are smashing.

Our favourite film star is John Mills (1908–2005. He is in such thrilling films and boys everywhere cheer him on. *In Which We Serve* (1942) is about a British warship fighting the German Navy. The captain of the ship in the film (HMS *Torrin*) is Noel Coward (1899–1973). Mums talk a lot about him, but none of us know what they are talking about. A new film star is in this and his name is Richard Attenborough. They don't know if he'll come to anything, but we like him in this picture so we all hope he will.

John Mills is also in *We Dive at Dawn* (1944), in which he played a submarine captain after a German battleship, the *Brandenburg*. He got it of course and got back to base again. But it wasn't just war films that this great actor thrilled us with, as he was in *Great Expectations* (1946) with Jean Simmons (1929–

2010), and the awfully exciting film *Scott of the Antarctic* (1948). This one is gobbled up by hordes of boys, as we are all explorers at heart and Captain Scott's expedition was something we were taught at school, so to see a picture about it, and with our favourite film star as well, is perfect. He gets us all excited in pictures like *This Happy Breed* (1944) and *Waterloo Road* (1945) with another of our favourite actors, Stewart Granger (1913–93).

Other war pictures thrill us as well, such as *Convoy* (1940), *Coastal Command* (1942) and the exciting story of how the marvellous Spitfire was designed by Mr R.J. Mitchell, called *The First of the Few* (1942).

These pictures were good for us, but when love films were on it was only girls, mums and grannies that liked those. One they all made a fuss about was *Brief Encounter* (1945), which starred Trevor Howard (1913–88) and Celia Johnson (1908–82).

Ladies everywhere think this picture is wonderful, but we can't see why. Dragged along to see it, when all we really want to see is the supporting film, we have to sit through this and we nearly die of boredom. It is about a lady who goes to London and then gets a smut in her eye while waiting at a station for her train home. She's treated by a doctor who just happens to be there. What for? We get smuts in our eyes all the time. It's unavoidable when you're anywhere near a steam train. We don't need a doctor as our mums hook it out of our eyes with the corner of a handkerchief.

Well, anyway, they start up a friendship and go off to a flat in London somewhere. What for, we all want to know? What can they do there? Listen to the wireless or play snakes and ladders? The picture ends with this lady going home and her husband says, 'I'm glad you're back.' Well of course he is, who's going to get the family's tea if their mum doesn't come home on time? It's all slush as far as we're concerned. Bring on the war films and the smashing cowboy and Indian ones that are coming from America.

We're already thrilled to bits with films starring the famous singing cowboy Roy Rogers (1911–98), as well as Gene Autry (1907–98) and Hopalong Cassidy. This cowboy was played by actor William Boyd (1895–1972) but none of us ever call him that, he's always Hopalong to us. But now there's a great film called *Stagecoach* and this stars John Wayne (1907–79). It was made in America in 1939, and we all love it. John Wayne plays the Ringo Kid and he fights off all the Indians who are attacking the stagecoach. We've seen pictures with this big man in before, but they weren't very good. But *Stagecoach*, blimey, this is *Boy's Own* stuff.

Cinemas, as well as the top deck of a bus or tram, are always filled with smoke from cigarettes. Sitting watching a film you can see it drifting through the bright light coming from the projector. This never bothers us as most of our dads smoked at home too, and that filled at least one room.

Under cover of the darkness inside cinemas it is easy to perform the get in free trick. This means one or sometimes two boys going into the cinema and paying for their tickets. Once inside the auditorium these two creep behind the curtain that hides the fire doors and quietly open the doors. Then in come all the rest of their friends who were waiting outside. Whole gangs of boys and girls get in to see the films for free!

Radio

Listening to the wireless is something we do every night. Our favourite programme comes on at teatime (5–6 p.m.) so we usually get it before more bombs started falling. It was called *Children's Hour* and is a programme some of our parents listened to before we were even born, because it started way back in 1926. To sit down with our brothers and sisters and listen to such thrilling things as the *Just So Stories* by Rudyard Kipling (1865–1936), which are mostly about animals and how they came to be as they are, is wonderful. We hear why a whale has a small throat – because one swallowed a fisherman and he built a raft and blocked

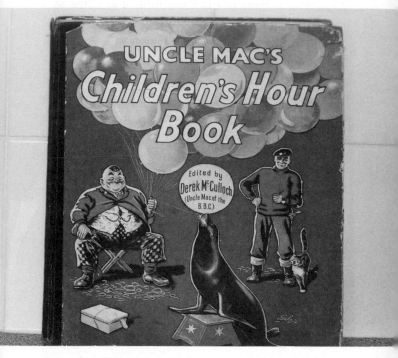

Cover of the *Children's Hour* annual.

the whale's throat with it so that it couldn't swallow any more men. Other explanations follow – how a camel got its hump, how a leopard got its spots and all sorts of stuff like that. We love these tales and most of us believe them as well.

The Sherlock Holmes stories by Sir Arthur Conan Doyle (1859–1930) are simply smashing. After every one of these, roads and school playgrounds everywhere has someone pretending to be the great detective. Boys go around with home-made deerstalker hats (mums and grannies are pressed into service to make these out of any old material they can find, and some of them look nothing like the ones that were described on the wireless), a piece of wood dangling from the mouth, supposed to be the pipe Holmes always smoked, and a small magnifying glass out of a Christmas cracker from before the war. With these, the famous detective sets to work to track down the villains. Funny how they never caught anyone though.

We love to listen to *Worzel Gummidge*. Being town kids we have never seen a scarecrow, but these stories about one who comes to life and gets into all sorts of funny situations that even we can't get up to are hilarious. He has three heads that he changes to suit whatever task he is trying to do; there's his turnip head, his mangel-wurzel head and his swede head. He falls in love with a fairground doll called Aunt Sally and gets into trouble because of that.

The evacuated kids have the chance to listen to these stories as well, of course, but they can then go outside and actually see real scarecrows. Standing in fields, the scarecrows frighten off the birds to stop them from eating the seeds that farmers sowed to grow wheat.

They country kids also have a better chance than us of playing pooh sticks. The idea for this came from the stories on *Children's Hour* about a honey-loving bear called Winnie the Pooh by Mr A.A. Milne (1882–1956). This bear, also known as Pooh Bear, played the stick game, and it was an easy thing to do. Everyone playing finds a stick then a bridge they can stand on. All of them throw their stick into the water then rush to the other side of the bridge to see which stick has gone under first, then holds its position until the end of the track, usually a bend in the stream. On the wireless the game is played properly and the winner congratulated, but when we try this doesn't happen at all. Arguments break out over whose stick is whose, and anyone claiming the winner is suddenly surrounded by the rest and called a cheat. More than one kid ends up in the water because of this.

In 1948 we all listen to a story about a boy and his best friend who go to a boarding school and this is a big hit. It is called *Jennings Goes to School* and it is hilarious. This story was written by a man called Anthony Buckeridge (1912–2004). We were told that his stories about Jennings would soon be published so we could all read them. This doesn't happen until 1950 though. Jennings is a super kid and his best friend at Linbury Court Preparatory School is Darbishire. What a hoot it is listening to the things these two, and the rest of the boys in their class, got up to.

Children's Hour, though it is only on for half an hour a day for part of the war, is something we all look forward to every day. We can forget about what is happening all around us and just let our imaginations run away as we sit on the floor in front of the old wireless set. These stories are read for us by a man called David McCulloch (1897–1967), whom we all knew as Uncle Mac. In Scotland, at the same time, kids listen to the same stories read by Kathleen Garscadden (1897–1991) and they know her as Auntie Kathleen.

There are other things for families to listen to, and sometimes we are allowed to stay up for them – as long as there isn't another air raid of course. We like the show starring Tommy Handley (1892–1949) that started in 1939, called *ITMA* (*It's That Man Again*). We laugh such a lot at this because it makes fun of Adolf Hitler as well as the German war effort. A film of this show is made in 1942 and it is just as funny.

Towards the end of the war, in 1944, a new show starts that we all listen to called *Much Binding in the Marsh*. It stars a man we haven't heard of before called Kenneth Horne (1907–69). It is about an RAF station in a place called Much Binding, and one of our favourite stars, Richard Murdoch, is in this as well. the whole family laughs at this programme every time it comes on and Mr Horne is soon well known by everybody. It is on the wireless for ten years, until 1954.

One thing we aren't supposed to hear are the messages coming out of Germany from a bloke from Ireland, known all over Britain as Lord Haw Haw. He is a traitor as far as our people are concerned and he sends out what our mums call propaganda messages, always telling us the Germans are winning the war and we haven't a hope against them. We, of course, don't understand what a bad thing this is for someone to do, but as we lie in bed we can hear what he says every time. What amuses us is the start of his broadcasts, when he says, 'Germany Calling, Germany Calling'. He has such a funny accent that it sounds like 'Gairmany Calling'. What a hoot!

In 1947, the comedy duo Jimmy Jewel (1909–95) and Ben Warris (1909–93) appear in a show called *Up the Pole*. These two are compared a lot with the American comedians Bud Abbot and Lou Costello, who are also popular. We see them in some films that have come over here and they are funny, but Jewel and Warris are English and we like them more because of that. They make us laugh as we listen to them and, as your mum says, 'there's no substitute for laughter'.

Also in 1946, the very exciting serial *Dick Barton* starts. Dick is a special agent and he has two sidekicks, Snowy and Jock. These three battle against crooks who want to take over the world, and each night they end up in such a tight spot that it seems impossible for them to escape. But at 6.45 the next evening they miraculously get out of this position and go after the crooks again. Dick was played by Noel Johnson (1916–99) while Jock and Snowy were played by Alex McCringle (1911–90) and John Mann.

To our huge delight two films are made about Dick Barton in 1948 and 1949. The first of these is called *Dick Barton Special Agent* and the second one *Dick Barton Strikes Back*. We pack the picture houses to see these as soon as they come out. All through the war Adolf Hitler is responsible for children being either indoors or inside a shelter, but in peacetime the streets and woodlands of Great Britain are clear of children every weekday evening when the strains of the tune 'Devil's Gallop' (composed by Charles Williams) come out of the speakers of wirelesses everywhere and kids sit with open mouths listening to this evening's episode of *Dick Barton Special Agent*.

Parents, and of course aunties and grannies, like to listen to the big band music, and older brothers and sisters go dancing when they can. Dance halls in London and most of the big cities have big bands playing and the dance floors are packed, especially before D-Day when the American soldiers were over here. Ted Heath's band is popular because the music sounds like that of Glenn Miller, whom Ted Heath met and talked with when Miller was touring Britain in 1944. Stanley Black is another whose orchestra is heard a lot on the wireless and in the dance halls up and down the country. Other big names include Geraldo and his orchestra and Jack Hylton.

Glenn Miller is an American big band leader and his style has older boys and girls crowding the dance halls wherever he and his band were playing. When he comes over in 1944 he had the same effect on our people as well. He is on the wireless a lot, and even we kids loved listening to tunes like 'Little Brown Jug' and 'Chattanooga Choo Choo'. It is a big shock to us when the news comes that Mr Miller had left England in December 1944 to fly to France, but he never arrived. Nothing more is said about what happened to this man, so we never have any idea how he disappeared. It is thought, of course, that his plane was shot down by the Germans.

Clothes

The 1940s sees lots of different varieties of clothes, though for us it simply means wearing what your older brothers or other boys in your road have grown out of. While there is still wear in anything it is passed on in this way. Nothing is wasted. So for boys it means black shoes, long grey socks, short grey trousers that come to just above the knee, then either a white or grey shirt, hand-knitted pullover, a grey jacket and, on the head, if you're lucky, a matching cap. Some boys though, with mums and grannies who were good at knitting, have to put up with a balaclava. This goes right over the head and comes down to the neck, completely covering the head so only your face is still visible. Girls do better than us. They wear dresses, usually with a flower pattern on them, and ankle socks, a woollen cardigan and a ribbon in their hair. A lot of them have pigtails, so a ribbon is tied to the end of each one of these.

Boys and girls have one lot of clothes that has to be worn on Sundays. Girls actually look nice when dressed in their Sunday best dresses, with brightly coloured ribbons keeping their hair in place. We have matching short trousers and jackets and we have to wear a tie, like our dads, when going to church. On these occasions our shoes are polished by our mums until they gleam, but once church is over and we are let out to play the shoes are the first to suffer. No red-blooded British boy ever comes home without that necessary sign of boyhood, scuffed shoes. Older girls wear dresses or sometimes skirts, and they go to somewhere called a salon to have their hair permed.

The boy gazing into the newsagent's window in Kent is dressed as all boys of that time were – black shoes, long socks, short trousers with a shirt and jacket. The boy walking down the road with an older lady has the regulation cap on his head. (War and Peace Archives)

On their feet they wear shoes with a very high heel and, of course, those stockings with the thin line down the back. They had to draw the line on their legs during the war.

Older boys we call spivs, because of the suits they wear, bought with a cheque from the provident mostly: black shoes, long black trousers and matching jacket, worn with a white shirt and black tie. Sometimes the suits are a different colour but they are the same design and older boys think they look great in them. We laugh at them (when they aren't looking,

This is the kind of suit worn by men who were considered to be gentlemen. This is Ian Bayley of the 1940s Society. (Penny Legg)

of course) because we think they look silly, especially when they plaster their hair down with Brylcreem.

At home, mums wear dresses with a pinafore over them and a headscarf. They do this to keep the hair out of their eyes while they do the housework. Grannies do this a lot as well, though their dresses are longer than the ones mums wear. But in the evenings when your mum leaves you in the care of your gran so she can go out for the evening, she too wears stockings. She does her hair up nicely and puts on lipstick, like your sisters use. This isn't easy to get during the war and girls everywhere have to make do as best they can. But in peacetime, places like Woolworths sell lipstick and girls put it all over their lips to make them come up bright red. They paint their nails as well, so that when they are dressed up most of what you can see has been painted on. Thank goodness boys don't have to do all this. One thing none of us can understand is why when mums are ready to go out for the evening they put on a fox fur. Why a lady wants to go around with a dead fox round her neck none of us can explain, but they seem to think it looks great.

Granddads wear trousers and a shirt with a pullover and tie, but these always seem to be old and out of shape. At the seaside they roll their trousers up to their knees, and then knot a handkerchief and plonk this on top of their heads to keep off the sun. We all suppose this works alright, but blimey what a laugh we have when we know we can't be seen.

When they come home from the war, dads have a suit given to them and it is called a demob suit. Most of them come home still wearing the uniform of the army, navy or air force, but once they are back in work again it is back to the way things were before. They wear shirt and trousers with a jacket as well and many men also have a flat cap. Many of them, when getting home in the evening, stride into the parlour and place the cap on the nail behind the door, put there especially for this purpose. When they go out in the evening though, usually to the local pub, they wear a freshly ironed and starched white shirt, a suit and black shoes, some of them also sporting a flower in the buttonhole on the lapel of the jacket.

All in all we don't do so badly. All of us kids look forward to the one time each year when new clothes are bought for us. They are always too big so that we can grow into them, but boy what a treat when you can wear something that hasn't previously been owned by another kid.

Six

FOOD, DRINKS AND SWEETS

Every family, both during and after the war, is on rations, so you can only buy what you have got coupons for. Even then it's only what you're allowed each week. It's a swizz really because we're growing children and we need plenty of food, but Mr Churchill keeps telling us we must all pull together and make do if we are to survive and win. That's all very well for him. He hasn't got to wait for his turn to have part of the crust from a loaf of bread does he? Sometimes mum cuts all the crust off, then cuts it up and gives us children a piece each. This is a fair way, as kids will fight to get at the crust otherwise.

Butter is something none of us ever see, as dads and granddads have the little bit (2oz) we're allowed in our rations each week. For us it's either dripping or margarine. Jam can be bought in jars, and the cheapest of these is plum. Children eat this on their bread every night for tea, whilst many a cat has learned that bread and plum jam is all they're going to get as well.

Bread is sold to our mums the day after it's baked. We're told it's easier to cut thinly than when freshly baked, but surely it's not as tasty as it would be on the day it comes out of the oven? The idea is that we won't want to eat so much of it at a time then. Who are they kidding? We eat as much bread every day as our mums will let us, whether freshly baked or not. Mum cuts it thin to make each loaf go further, but at night she cuts it thicker so that we can toast it in front of the kitchen range before spreading it with margarine or dripping.

When shopping, the ration book is placed on the counter. The shopkeeper then puts up our family's rations and we have to take whatever the shop has got in stock that week. Mums can't say, 'No, I'd rather have another brand than this please,' because the shop simply hasn't got anything else in. Stuff that is used for puddings is also very hard to get. One way of filling children's stomachs is to give them large helpings of suet puddings, especially if there are any sultanas to put in them to make spotted dick. But suet, like everything else, is in such short supply that your mum has to save points to get it. She gets these from the grocer's shop, and when there are enough, along with coupons to go with them, she can buy suet.

While she is saving the points, though, these puddings are made with flour. Instead of suet, potato is used as a substitute. The whole thing is then wrapped in a cloth and boiled in the same way. It's funny really, we don't even notice any difference. They look just the same as the suet ones and with lots of custard, made with powdered milk, the whole thing is eagerly eaten and it sure does fill us up.

Another thing that is home-made is chocolate spread, from margarine, sugar and cocoa. This is spread on bread and tastes really good. In the larder there are always things like tins of spam or corned beef. These can be used to make meals or sandwiches. It's easier to keep these because they are in tins so there is no need to keep them in the meat safe. Some mums and older sisters use the powdered milk to make batter and then slice up the meat. They then dip the slices in the batter before frying them on the gas stove. Spam or corned beef fritters are just super-duper blooming smashing when you get them with chips on your plate.

The average family ration of food during the war is: 4oz bacon, 8oz sugar, 2oz tea, 1lb of meat or up to 1s 2d worth a week, 2oz cheese, 2oz butter, 4oz margarine, 2oz lard (for cooking), one egg and one packet of dried egg every two months. It doesn't seem a lot when it's put like that, and we often wonder how our mums can put great dinners up for us all every day of the week. Okay we only have one cooked meal a

Rations for one family had to last a whole week before more could be bought. (War and Peace Show 2013)

day and we make do with bread and dripping or toast the rest of the time, but that one cooked meal is so special. Some children from poorer families have free school dinners, so for five days a week they get their one cooked meal that way.

We hear that Mr Churchill saw a picture of the average family's rations and said, 'Well, this looks like a decent enough meal to me.' It was then pointed out that this much food had to last the family for a whole week, not just for one meal. He understood then what a struggle people were having trying to feed whole families on just this small amount of food. Soap is also rationed. We don't mind that, but mums still seem to manage to get enough of that hard Sunlight soap to make our lives a misery on bath nights.

Our concern is how we buy our sweets, because these are rationed as well and we have to be very careful when going to the shop. It's not just the price of sweets that is the worry but how many precious coupons it takes to get a quarter of toffees or dolly mixtures. We can earn pocket money from the sale of horse manure or running errands for neighbours. But mums keep warning us about the coupons. 'Be careful with those,' she says, 'because once they're gone there won't be any more until the next lot of ration books are issued.' This only took place every three months. So we have to decide whether to take the whole ration book so that the shopkeeper can cut the coupons out of this, or have your mum cut one or two coupons to take with you. There were things to worry about either way. If you take the whole ration book, you have to be careful not to lose it because the coupons for the rest of the things the family needs are in there as well. Also there is the added nuisance of having to go home to take the book back before running off to play. If you take the coupons your

Copper coins were very familiar, as were the threepenny bit and the sixpenny piece.

mum has cut out for you, they are so small that it's easy to lose them and that would be a tragedy.

Boys love to buy things that will last a long time and for a penny each we got gobstoppers. These are so big they fill our mouths, so that for quite a long time none of us could even speak. They start to dissolve as we suck on them, and a different colour comes through with a different taste as well. It is funny really, because we still play together without any of us being able to shout out as we usually would. Gobstoppers put a stop to that! They last for ages, though, and are well worth the money we pay for them. Not many girls buy these; they were not very ladylike. The ones known as tomboys, because they like to do the same things as boys, do have the cheek to copy us with these sweets, but most girls enjoy more girly sweets such as dolly mixtures. We get these as well because they go further when we share them out.

Other sweets we all love are acid drops, mint hum-bugs and aniseed balls. These taste great and turn your tongue bright red when you suck on them. We also like liquorice comfits and liquorice allsorts, toffees ,and, when we can get them, barley sugar sweets. We get Black Jack chews that taste like aniseed and turn your tongue black. Beech-Nut chewing gum is also a big favourite with us all.

A lot of evacuees were sent to a county called Yorkshire and when they come back, the ones from our town tell us about the pursuit camp called Bewerley Park, which was near a village called Pateley Bridge. There's a sweet shop there that's the oldest one in England. It has been there since 1827, way before our granddads were even born. The evacuated children loved this shop and the kindly people who owned it and came down every week to spend their few pennies pocket money. The liquorice sticks were popular because the liquorice was grown locally. We just thought liquorice was made the same way as all other sweets and didn't know anything about this. Other boiled sweets filled the big glass jars, lined up all along the shelves, so it was difficult sometimes to make up your mind what to buy this week.

We hear of boys who lived in this lovely village and one in particular who used to run errands for his granny. She gave him a penny for doing this and he would then rush off to this wonderful old shop. Here he bought sweets and came out with halfpenny change. This was then spent in the local fish and chip shop, where he got a big bag of scraps. Wow, give any

The lovely village of Pateley Bridge in Yorkshire. (The Oldest Sweet Shop in England)

The Oldest Sweet Shop in England, in Pateley Bridge High Street. (The Oldest Sweet Shop in England)

Stepping inside this fascinating shop is just like stepping back in time. This is how all sweet shops looked in the 1940s, with rows of jars on the shelves all containing mouth-watering sweets. As long as you had money and sweet coupons you could spend time picking out the ones you wanted to buy. (The Oldest Sweet Shop in England)

of us the chance to invade this shop and none of us would have any trouble picking out what we wanted.

The kids who were sent to Bewerley Park came from Leeds and they found that life there was so much better than the one they knew at home. Well, they had a bathroom for a start. They all slept in dormitory huts, boys and girls separated as usual. But the bathroom was better in so many ways to the tin bath we all have to use, with hot water that doesn't have to be heated in a copper – a luxury we didn't have. There is a drawback of course: this bath holds at least twenty kids at a time. Well you have to make some sacrifices, don't you?

One of the girls who went there told us about it afterwards. It was important to get to the front of the queue for the bath, because then you could claim a place near the taps. The ones at the other end had to put up with cold water because by the time it got to that end the heat had simply gone from it. But they had the advantage of this sweet shop just a mile down the road from the camp.

We can also get one-penny chews and they cost just what the name says and so are a penny (1*d*) each. The smaller ones are half as much and cost a half-penny. They taste of different fruit flavours, and as they cost so little we can buy more of them at a time, when we have any money to spend. We like sherbet lemons, which are boiled sweets with sherbet inside. What a dream this is as you suck the sweet until it dissolves and get to the delicious part in the middle. In places like Yorkshire sherbet is known as kali, but whatever it's called it tastes great. We children have yellow tongues each time they suck on these sweets.

Toffee came in big slabs and the man in the sweet shop had a small hammer that he used to break this up if we wanted to buy any of it. We did this sometimes but not anywhere near as often as some of the other sweets, because toffee cost more in both money and coupons. One of our favourite chocolate bars was

Fry's Five Boys. When we did manage to buy a bar it was such a dream as we sat in our camps and shared it out. It was lovely milk chocolate and on the wrapper were the faces of five boys, just like us. Mars bars are something all children loved but during this time of rationing we can only ever buy one bar each time we go to the sweet shop. This is because they are in such short supply – it is something to do with the stuff that was inside. The factories can't get enough of the stuff they needed to make these famous bars so they are strictly rationed. Oh well, we can't really afford them anyway.

We love fizzy drinks and one of our favourites is Corona. Mums can buy different flavours such as lemonade, limeade, cherryade and dandelion and burdock. The bottles have special stoppers that are worked by a metal spring that makes it go back tightly into the top. Because of this there is money on the bottle, so we get as many at a time as we can and then take them back to the shop. The few pennies we get in return are spent on sweets. These drinks were brought round to the door by a man with a horse and cart before the war, but so many of these blokes are eventually called up to fight that the rounds were discontinued and we have to buy the drinks from shops. Afterwards though, these Corona rounds begin again. Tizer is another of our favourites, a red fizzy drink that most of us have.

Being kids we make our own drinks, and for this we use lemonade powder or sherbet. This is mixed up with water and it is good enough for us all to enjoy. Girls as well as boys do this because it is easy and cheap. We like to dip liquorice sticks into this powder, as well, and then suck it off the end.

We drink tea at home and cocoa at bedtime, but some of the grown-ups like to have coffee as well. This comes in a bottle and is called Camp Coffee. We've tried it ourselves and it's awful. How can anyone drink something that tastes as bad as this? But granddads everywhere as well as mums and grannies like it. They have it at night while they listen to the wireless. It's made with hot milk, which means the powdered stuff, so that's probably why we all hate it so much. We get real milk at school and we drink it at morning playtime. Sometimes this means running to the shelter first and drinking the milk down there as explosions go on over our heads.

There's another treat we all enjoy as well, the same as the boy in Yorkshire, and that is a bag of scraps from the fish and chip shop. This is batter that has broken off in the fat as the fish fries, and these bits are scooped out by the shopkeeper. It builds up and most of these shops are only too pleased to reward us when we turn up with a load of newspapers for them to wrap the fish and chips in so customers can carry them home. We get a whopping great bag of scraps to share out between us, and many boys run back to their bomb-site camps to enjoy this treat.

The slogan 'Dig for Victory' was something everyone took notice of. As much food as possible needed to be grown to feed us all. Land girls of course worked on farms and planted things like potatoes and stuff that all of us needed. Some boys go on to the land to help when these are dug up. They have to be picked up and thrown into a cart that is drawn by a big horse before the whole lot is taken back to the farm that owned the land. Phew, that must be hard work. But most people are being urged to turn their gardens into mini farms and grow as much stuff as they can. One story we all thought was a hoot was about a lady who really took this to heart and while her husband was away dug up their front lawn to plant potatoes. When her husband came home he was horrified to see that the lawn that he had spent so much time keeping neat and tidy had disappeared. This normally happy couple went through a time of great strain after this because that lawn had been the husband's pride and joy. He wouldn't have given it up for anybody, not even because someone had started a blooming war.

Seven

School Life

In school, especially while the war is on, we have classes of over forty children at a time in the towns and cities. The country schools aren't much better as they now have loads of evacuated children doubling the numbers in their classes. Most of the teachers are ladies, as the men have all been called up to fight the Germans. The only men in schools up until the end of the war in 1945 are caretakers and they are the same age as our granddads, really old men.

For younger children, born from 1940 onwards, beginning school is something that can only be described as torture. While the war is on these young kids have been with their mothers all the time and, like us before them, told the things that are important as they grow up. Don't take sweets from someone you don't know and never accept rides from a stranger.

This makes sense of course, but our mums would have a fit if they could see us as we walk to school each day. After the Americans have come into the war, we looked out for Yankee soldiers and then the cry of 'Got any gum, chum?' goes up. These men may be strangers to us, but they're on our side in this war, and all of them have got gum and chocolate as well.

Small children are watched closely by their mothers. As a result they fail to meet others of their own age, except in the shelters or down in the Underground during yet another air raid, but they also go nowhere without having to hold tightly to their mother's hand. Then, quite suddenly, they are taken to a very large hall where rows and rows of clothes are hanging up on rails. In this large place, once their mum has shown she has enough coupons, a new suit of clothes is bought for her small son or daughter. For boys it is a matching jacket and short trousers in grey, with a pair of long socks, black shoes and a cap. Girls get a dress. Boys and girls get an overcoat as well, and a mackintosh to keep out the rain.

Then, dressed well, they go to a building that looks like something out of a Charles Dickens book. Inside here, along with loads more kids the same age as them, they have the horror of seeing their mothers walking away and leaving them in this horrible place. Most of them tried to run after their mothers but are stopped

Photographs and descriptions of boys' clothes appear a lot throughout this book. These two girls in a garden in Kent show what young ladies wore during this period. The girl on the right is wearing the traditional flower-patterned dress, while her companion is wearing a plain one. Both have ankle socks and a hat. (War and Peace Archives)

A mixed class with boys sharing desks with girls. This was almost unheard of during the 1940s, and even in this photograph there is a gap between the boy and the girl. In the bottom far-left corner the boy in the black blazer grew up to become the celebrated crime writer Peter Lovesey. (Peter Lovesey)

by the teachers and pushed into a classroom. This is the beginning of school life in Britain in the 1940s.

For us, though, it is business as usual with games in the playground and lessons in between. It soon gets back to how it was before the war, except we are now lumbered with taking our small brothers and sisters to school each day and getting them safely back home again in the evenings. From 1940 until 1945 we had been taught mainly by ladies, because all of the men were in the forces. They were good at teaching and they were also just as good with a cane or a ruler as any man. We never got away with bad behaviour because it meant that cane coming down on to our hands or the ruler hitting the back of these or the back of our knees.

We all love to play tricks on the old caretaker before school starts each day. Because he is so old it is easy to tell him things that aren't true and hide his buckets and mops. We all think this is such a hoot – until our lady teacher tells us what these old men get up to in the evenings.

Standing in front of the class she says:

I have noticed how you all make fun of old Mr Jacobs the school caretaker. I know you all think he is funny because he is old, but I think it's about time you were told what he and a lot of other men his age are doing in the evenings, and through the night. Mr Jacobs takes his turn at fire watching. This means he stands on top of the tallest buildings in this city and watches the bombs falling. Once an incendiary explodes into a raging fire he calls in and tells the fire brigade where it is, so that they can get there quickly to try and put it out. This is very dangerous work and many men are killed when the building they are standing on is hit. Most of them fought for this country in the first war and now they are taking up arms again in the Home Guard. Make no mistake, if the Germans ever do invade this country, Mr Jacobs, and a lot of men his age, will fight to keep it free from Nazi occupation.

Boys in a classroom at a school in Kent during a gas mask drill. (War and Peace Archives)

Many a caretaker must wonder why we are all polite to him now – it's because we know how brave he is.

Lessons take place in classrooms that have very little heating. There are pipes around the bottom of the walls that give out some heat, but in the winter this isn't really enough. Boys usually sit two at a desk and the girls do the same. It's never one boy and one girl. There's an invisible wall built between us so that boys and girls rarely mix, even though we are all in the same class. Most schools won't even let us play together, and the girls have a playground and entrance on one side whilst the boys have their playground and entrance on the opposite side.

Lessons are divided up as well, so the boys do woodwork and metalwork, while the girls do cookery and sewing. This is because boys will be dads when they grow up and will need these skills to be able to work and get the money they need for their families. The girls are taught to do housework because they'll grow up to be mums and housewives. No girl ever sets foot in either the woodwork room or the class-rooms where metalwork is done. These are boys only. We, of course, never set foot in or go anywhere near the cookery or needlework rooms.

Playgrounds are surrounded by railings that keep us all in and safe from anyone outside. There is a shed in both the girls' and boys' playgrounds where we can all go to keep dry when it rains, but we love to be out in it. What does it matter if we all get wet? Lots of us stand with faces turned up to the sky so that the rain runs down it then on to our outer clothes as well. This is fun, but our teachers don't understand and they shout at us for it.

The girls play netball in their playground because it has a better surface. We've watched them playing and can't understand what the game is all about. Each girl

Boys in a school in Kent take part in a woodwork lesson. This is typical of the way this was done during this decade of war and peace. Two boys shared one bench and they both had a cupboard where tools were kept. (War and Peace Archives)

stops once they get the ball before they pass it to one of the other players. How daft. We would run with the ball bouncing it as we go, then, once in a shooting position, throw it through the hoop at the top of the pole to score a goal. The girls should watch us as we play shinty in our playground. This is a version of hockey, played with smaller sticks and at a much faster rate. The sticks are just the right size to hook around an opponent's ankles and trip them up to stop them getting away with the ball. Our games masters shout at us when we do this, bellowing, 'I've told you before not to use your shinty sticks to trip an opponent.' Our answer of, 'Sorry, Sir, it was an accident,' is never accepted, and the school nurse tells us off too when we go to her afterwards to have plasters on our grazed knees.

In the classrooms we have inkwells in both corners of the desks and a lid that opens up so we can get to the books and things that are kept in there. Well, that's what's supposed to be in the desks. But, boys being boys there are other things as well, the odd frog, or large moth, and if you can get one, a mouse. These are smuggled into the desks of the girls before the teacher comes into the classroom, and sometimes into her desk as well. What a hoot this is as all of them, teacher as well, scream the place down when they see these creepy crawlies. If we're caught though it's the cane, and boy do they lay it on.

Girls also suffer the ink trick, where boys sitting behind them gently take hold of the ends of their hair and dip it into the inkwell. If the unfortunate girl has pigtails, both ends are treated. They get into awful trouble when they get home because their mothers have a fit when they see them. They are supposed to be clean and tidy at all times, which is why they also don't pick things up from the ground like we do.

Another trick with ink is done by the lucky person, usually a boy, who gets the much sought-after job of ink monitor. They get time off lessons so they can go round with a big jug full of ink and fill all of the classroom's inkwells. Coming to the desk of a boy or girl who has done something this person doesn't like, especially if it causes them to be punished for a misdemeanour, the ink monitor will deliberately pour ink along the top of the desk where the hinges for the lid run. In this way it seeps inside the desk and goes all over the books and papers inside.

Writing has to be done neatly and without ink blots, but most of us find this impossible. We have wooden sticks with a nib on the end of them that we have to use as pens. So once you dip these flipping things into the inkwell the nib picks up more than it needs and has a horrible habit of dripping off and causing blots. We get caned for this, which isn't fair really because it isn't our fault the ink keeps dripping off, is it? One thing we do, though, is make sure we have blotting paper handy so you can at least soak up most of the blot that way. This paper has to be guarded during lessons as some boys have a nasty habit of pinching it if they don't have any of their own.

This was the only use for blotting paper, of course. None of us well behaved boys would dream of tearing little bits of this off the main sheet, rolling it up then pushing it into the inkwell so that it becomes soaked with ink, then using our rulers to shoot this inky missile at other pupils in the class. Would we do such a thing? Of course we would, and a lot of us are dead shots at this. Man boys and girls go home with ink marks on their necks and behind their ears.

Some children have to move around a lot, as their fathers do important work for the armed forces. They go to whatever schools are in the area before moving on again. Boys simply get on with it and attend the various schools, but some of the girls also have to help their mothers with housework, shopping and stuff in towns where they don't know anyone. We hear later of a girl who lands up in South London for a while because her granddad had a shop there. This area would become well known in the 1960s as the head-quarters of the notorious Richardson Gang. Wow, if we had known that at the time we would have been over the moon. We all love watching gangster films with American actors like James Cagney (1899–1986), Humphrey Bogart (1899–1957), Edward G. Robinson (1893–1973) and George Raft (1901–80) in them.

There are stories of schools that make children bring teaspoons with them, which are then used to shovel malt into their mouths every morning. These spoons are then laid on newspaper and the children collect them at home time. Some kids that aren't fast enough in joining the queue as all the children leave the building, find, to their horror, that all of the spoons have already gone, others having picked up more than one. A lot of mums are very upset when their offspring comes home spoonless.

All of us have to learn things like aircraft recognition; after all, we need to know whether a plane flying overhead is one of ours or an enemy that could drop a bomb on us at any time. In the classrooms we have posters of objects we aren't supposed to pick up. These include milk bottles, lemonade bottles and all sorts of stuff like that. It was because those Germans are dropping bombs that look just like these everyday things and if they are picked up then they will go off. How mean can they get?

While the war is on we are allowed to go out on to the playing fields for games, but always have to make sure we have gas masks with us. If the siren sounds then we have to run back quickly into school to get into the shelter before the bombs start falling. Once it's all over games can be played properly again. Football, cricket and rounders for the boys. Netball in the winter on the playground for the girls, while in summer they play rounders outside. For these sports boys change into black shorts and white vests, so we look alright. But on the sports field all the girls have their blouses tucked into the most horrible blue knickers. We think they looked ghastly in those and the girls aren't very happy with them either.

In infants and secondary modern school we all wear our own clothes. Our mums make sure they're as clean and smart as she can make them. So for us it's the same as our younger brothers: short grey trousers, matching long socks with black shoes, a white or grey shirt, pullover and a tie which we take off as soon as school is over for the day. We wear a jacket and a cap is plonked on our heads. Girls wear dresses with flowery patterns on them, or a skirt with a white blouse, white ankle socks and usually black shoes. They often have woollen cardigans, and all of them have a ribbon in their hair. Most of these clothes have been handed down by older children, but if new ones are needed mums use a cheque from the Provident to buy them.

For children who pass the scholarship, later the 11-plus, things are very different. They go on to grammar schools and for this they have to wear school uniform. These cost a lot and mums everywhere struggle to find the money to buy them. But they manage it, somehow, because they are so proud of their sons and daughters who have been clever enough to pass this exam.

Discipline in schools is strict, and misbehaviour of any sort is not allowed. Even whispering to someone in class means the cane being used. When the war was on the lady teachers were good with the cane and ruler, and used them both. But when the men come back another hazard is upon us – the accurate throwing of chalk, and sometimes the blackboard duster, at miscreants who are not paying attention in class. To be hit by either of these is not something any of us liked. Their aim is so good. We think their army training is the reason for this and we hardly have time to get out of the way of these flying objects.

But we're British boys aren't we? Practice makes perfect and after school in our secret bombsite camps we practise endlessly, throwing things at each other and having to dodge quickly to avoid being hit. This soon pays off so that chalk and dusters fly through the air and hit no one. We still get caned though, we don't get away with it. What a swizz that is.

And of course arriving late at school means punishment, usually from the Headmaster, so excuses for lateness are something all of us have to be experts at. 'Sorry, Sir, but I missed the tram, Sir,' is a good one but it is used such a lot that we rarely, if ever, get away with it. If you come to school on your bike excuses are easier.

One boy went to a school where the headmaster would always notice latecomers and challenge them straight away for the reason, in front of the whole school. He nearly made a king-size hash of it. When shouted at to reveal why he was late he answered, 'Sorry, Sir, but I had a puncture.' The head however didn't hear him and shouted, 'What did you say boy? Speak up.' In a panic now, the unfortunate lad shouted back, 'The chain on my bike broke, Sir.' The rest of the assembled children of course thought this was enormously funny and immediately burst into laughter. The boy with the mixed up excuses used this noise as a cover to lose himself with the rest of the children in the school hall.

But riding to school during the war years has its share of danger too. There are stories of children suddenly having to jump off and lie on the ground or dive into the nearest cover as fighter planes fly over and strafe the roads with bullets. To be hit by any of these would mean the boy or girl being killed.

School dinners are something we all think we're given as a punishment, because nothing should taste as awful as they do. Mums give us the money on Mondays for a week's school meals, and we have to hand this to our teachers. But the food is cooked in a kitchen somewhere else and transported in steel canisters to the various schools. This may be alright when it's first cooked, but by the time it gets to your school, and eventually on to your plate, it's been sitting in that canister for so long that it tastes awful. Meat, roast potatoes and cabbage should be smashing to eat – well the meat and potato anyway, not many boys like cabbage – but in the school canteen it tastes horrible. And we have to eat it because the teacher on dinner duty is watching so we don't dare leave any. We don't have any choices either. Whatever is being served we have to have on our plates, whether we like it or not. For many of us this is a trial, as we have milk puddings like tapioca. We call this frogspawn because that's what it looks like, and it tastes like it as well.

In the later years of the 1940s schools in other countries such as New Zealand send parcels of food that are then shared out to pupils in this country. What a thrill it is if you are lucky enough to be handed a tin of peaches or spam that you then carry home in triumph and give to your mother. It is such a help to our mothers, who still have to queue for hours at the shops to buy the rationed stuff even though the war is over. It doesn't always work out well, though, as some children are unlucky enough to always get the same thing each time these parcels arrive. One girl would always go home with a packet of pastry mix. This is a good thing to have, of course, but the girl in question would have simply loved to be able to carry a tin of ham or even spam home to her mother.

Sometimes, especially in places like London and many of the industrial towns in the north of England, children are sent home early because of the dense fog that suddenly comes down and makes seeing where you are going nearly impossible. This is caused by smoke from factory chimneys and now with the bombing going on all the time the situation is much worse. Even we kids, with our eagle eyes, have a job to see in these thick fogs, so even crossing roads is a dangerous thing to have to do.

So, the food is horrible, the discipline really hard, and the cane used every day on boy's hands to punishing effect. But, like our parents, we simply make the best of it.

Eight

SCHOOL HOLIDAYS

Throughout the war and afterwards, holidays are longed-for breaks in the monotony of the routine, both in school and at home: having to carry your gas mask everywhere, and doing exactly as your parents or teachers tell you to do. But at Easter, and the glorious six weeks' summer break, the world opens up for us and boy do we take advantage.

Now we can devote so much more of our time to collecting paper and old metal things to help our side in the war, and of course, looking for that precious shrapnel. And if a German plane has crashed anywhere near we can at least go and have a look at it. The regular soldiers or Home Guard men that are standing watch glare at us and dare us to even try coming too close. That's alright, because just looking at these wrecked planes with the German markings on the wings sends such a thrill through us. It may be, of course, that the men who were flying these planes were killed when it crashed, but we aren't thinking of this as we gaze at the twisted metal of what such a short time ago had been a German bomber plane that was here to try and drop more bombs on us. The fact it was shot down is another feather in the cap of our soldiers.

We can also play our own version of war, so it's off to the nearest wooded area where there is a river or stream big enough for us to wade across. We've seen soldiers doing this on Pathé News at the fleapit cinemas where we all go to watch the pictures. They simply wade into the water with their uniforms on and sometimes have to cross while under fire from the Germans. So we do that as well. Our play clothes get wet of course, but that's just part of the game. We divide up into British or German soldiers and the war is on. We fight each other as we run through the woods and once at the river the British troops jump straight in and start wading across. The Germans then arrive and start pelting us with stones or lumps of wood as we struggle in the water and eventually make it to the opposite bank. Then it's the enemy's turn to enter the water in order to keep the attack going, so they jump in too. Well, it's only fair – we're all wet so they can get wet too.

It ends of course with our clothes hanging from the branches of the trees to dry while we all enjoy ourselves swimming in the river. Girls are not allowed anywhere near while we're doing this. They swim as well, but at other parts of the river, and they post a lookout when they do this so that we can't get even a peak at what they look like when they're undressed. A girl's body is a mystery for us all and we wonder if it's one that will ever be solved.

When we play in wooded areas girls like to join us, and some of them are alright, as long as they can keep up with us as we run and climb trees. But such a lot of them are useless at this. Their tree climbing is terrible. They jump at the bang made when we shoot our cap guns (whenever we can get the caps). They're hopeless at fighting and their swordplay is non-existent. So what good are girls then, apart from playing mums or nurses? They do join us when we play chasing games in the roads, having to jump over rubble and stuff and racing round and round the big shelters. We try and join them when they're skipping but this just gives them a chance to laugh at us as we always mess this up. How can they skip so fast, sometimes six at a time, and never get their feet tangled up in the rope? But we all enjoy hopscotch and we can play this as well as any of the girls.

Some families, mostly after the war, are able to go away on holiday for a week, or sometimes two. Mums save up the money each week so that once the summer holidays begin she has enough to take her children away to the seaside. For kids born as the war started, 1946 is the first time many of them have even been outside of the town or city where they were born. During the first part of the 1940s, the railways are crowded with soldiers, sailors and airmen moving from one place to another. Families have to squeeze in and spend an uncomfortable time in the trains before they reach their stop. Kids of course make light of this, and thoroughly enjoy riding on a train and going to another place altogether. During the first part of the 1940s the seaside is not somewhere any of us can go to, because of the defences. If any Germans did get across the Channel and try to take over our country there would be a very nasty surprise waiting for them on our beaches. All of these, from the south coast resorts of Bournemouth, Brighton, Weymouth, Portsmouth and Southsea down into Devon and Cornwall are treated to the same sort of defences. Up country, as well, the beaches in famous places such as Blackpool, Cleethorpes, Margate, Scarborough, Morecombe, Whitby, Worthing, and anywhere else the Germans could land, are mined. Barbed wire fences prevent civilians going on to the beaches and getting blown up by our own mines. That's alright with us, because none of us wants to step on one, do we? Places with piers, such as Southend, had these blocked off for the same reason, so no joy for us there, either.

A seaside holiday after the end of the Second World War. This photograph shows the author's family on the beach at Bournemouth in 1947. The angelic little boy, second from the right, is the author, aged 6.

But one thing put into place gives us endless hours of fun after the war, the large chunks of concrete that were tank stoppers. Boys spend hours with these, jumping from one to the next at speed, the object being to get to the last one of these large concrete blocks without falling off. Anyone who does fall ends up being comforted by his mum as she bathes his badly grazed knees before putting either a bandage or a plaster on them.

But the second half of the 1940s is a treat, as we can get back to enjoying ourselves and go to the seaside. Sometimes, well most times actually, this is just for the day. But it is such a wonder, especially for the young kids who hadn't been anywhere outside of the place where they were born, to suddenly be travelling on something as exciting as a steam train. Children from London are taken to Brighton with its magnificent beaches and this is a thrill. For most of them it is the first time they have actually seen the sea, although they have of course grown up within the area of the most famous river in England, the Thames.

Young children have never seen things like horses, sheep and cows that they can now see from the train window. Once on the beach it's getting into your bathers under a towel your mum has wrapped round you – no mean feat because if it drops before you get them on then the embarrassment is awful. But once you're ready you can introduce your younger brothers and sisters to bathing in the sea. They shriek with delight as the waves come in and you lift them up as the water rushes past. The beaches are so crowded with families from all over the country flocking to them. The youngsters build sandcastles and then all of us take turns riding the donkeys. With Punch and Judy shows to enjoy as well, a day at the beach is quite simply smashing. Eating the sandwiches mum has brought for us is fun, even though a lot of sand seems to get into them.

Most of the small kids, as well as us, have never really travelled on anything other than the trams that run in their own towns. Some towns have buses, and places like Blackpool have trolley buses, but riding on a train that has comfortable seats and travels at speed no tram can get anywhere near is such an exciting event. The other way to travel to the seaside is by charabanc (coach). These go on the roads and they have comfortable seats as well.

All through the marvellous school summer holidays we forget about the harsh discipline of school and just concentrate on having a great time. This six-week holiday is the best because it's the longest, but we also have just as much fun at Easter, with fairs coming and setting up on grasslands near to our homes. Riding the bumper cars and the jungle ride means us boys can show off to the girls about how brave we are. This also happens at Whitsun (Spring Bank Holiday) and August Bank Holiday. Some families do go away together for at least a week, but others, and that certainly includes us, just go for day trips. For this mums have saved up all through the year so they can buy tickets on the railway and it's wonderful to get up in the morning and not knowing where you're going today.

It's not just the regular holidays that we love, but also the ones we shouldn't get, because the weather does us all a favour. In the winter of 1946–47 we have a 'big freeze', which is marvellous. Our schools are closed because of frozen pipes. Parents aren't very happy about this because the cisterns in our outside toilets freeze again and in some villages people are cut off and can't get to the shops because roads are blocked by snow. None of us children are bothered by this because we have a winter wonderland to play in. We can build snowmen and have wonderful snow-ball fights. We think the girls will be easy to pelt with these, but they soon show that they are just as good as any of us at this – blooming cheek, boys should be better than girls at everything! A lot of us are hit with snowballs thrown by them. So we sort things out by letting the girls join us in everything we do outside. We use our corrugated sheets to slide down steep banks that are now covered in snow. None of us have a real sledge, but these sheets of corrugated tin do just as good a job of sending us down these slopes at speed. Each boy has a girl sitting behind him and clinging on to his waist as they hurtle down and the screams of joy are deafening as the wind rushes past our ears.

We also have lakes and rivers near us, and when they freeze over it is such fun to go skating. First, though, a grown-up has to check that the ice is thick enough to hold our weight. There have been times when kids have gone skating only to find the ice is too thin when it starts to crack under their feet. Many

Children in Kent during the big freeze of 1946–47. None of them are bothered by the cold; they have already built a snowman and are now preparing for a snowball fight. (War and Peace Archives)

a boy has fallen through and had to be rescued quickly. If he is dragged out quickly everything is okay, but the unfortunate boy has to be taken straight home where his wet clothes can be taken off him. This is to make sure he doesn't go down with a bad cold or even worse. The water under the ice is freezing and the air out in the open is too, so anyone falling in has to be warmed up as quickly as possible. Once a grown-up has checked and given us the all clear it's out on to the ice. Gliding over the frozen surface of a pond or lake and getting up to speed is simply wonderful. Grown-ups come and join us as well, though they wear proper ice skates. We haven't got anything like that, because they cost too much and our mums can't afford them. But shoes with leather soles are just as good for skating across the ice, so boys and girls everywhere do it all the time. We take a run and then jump on to the surface, this then sends us racing across just as fast as anyone wearing ice skates and we think it's more fun doing it that way.

The big freeze begins in January 1947 and continues well into March. When the thaw eventually comes it brings more problems, with melting snow running into rivers and causing floods in many places. We aren't bothered about that, just disappointed that our wonderful winter wonderland holiday is ending and we have to go back to school. The grown-ups are happy that the big freeze was coming to an end. None of us agree with them about that.

But winter has another great treat for us when another holiday gets us out of school and into the winter weather. Some of us even have real sledges as Christmas presents, and others have footballs and things. Girls get new skipping ropes and all of us play outside, whatever the weather, and enjoy what Father

Christmas has brought for us. We get at least two weeks off school and all of us love it so much. Going back to school in the first week of January isn't something any of us look forward to, though.

When the children who were evacuated come back they tell us stories about their time away from their families and what they all got up to in their adopted homes. Many didn't have to wait for the school holidays in order to enjoy themselves, doing things they never did at home. They were in the country, so even at the height of the war they were taken by their teachers — sometimes their own teacher who had evacuated with them — to idyllic rivers and lakes where they could swim, go boating and fishing. Not all of them were as lucky, of course, and didn't enjoy being where they ended up. These kids were overjoyed when the war ended and they could go home to their parents again.

All in all though, British boys and girls never let a world war stop them from enjoying holidays in their great country, and nothing ever will.

Nine

CHRISTMAS

Christmas is the most exciting day of the year for children everywhere, and nothing is ever allowed to interfere with that. The build-up to this terrific day is so special, because we all know that somewhere up in the North Pole Father Christmas and his elves are getting all of the presents made, everything that we will find in the stockings that are hung up by the fireplace in the parlour, or on the end of our beds. But this year it's all so different because of this war.

Our mums have told us that Father Christmas probably won't be able to come now because it will be too dangerous for him and his reindeer. With all of the German bombers up in the sky, he won't be able to risk it. But we're also being told that Christmas will still be special for us – mums and grannies everywhere will make sure it is. Many of us will spend this special day in the air-raid shelters and Underground stations in London. Father Christmas can't get down there because there are no chimneys for him to climb down.

In other parts of England, whole families are celebrating inside the small Anderson shelters in their back gardens. Mums decorate the shelters and they look smashing. Only a very small Christmas tree will fit inside, so a big demand soon develops for these smaller trees. With such a small space inside, whole families have to crush together in order to squeeze in. Kids don't mind that though – as long as there are presents and sweets and things that we can't get during the year with all of us being rationed, Christmas, wherever it's spent, is magical.

What none of us know is that grown-ups are being told by the government not to buy presents this year, but to do something to help the war effort instead, so a lot of war bonds were bought. This means we have to make do with either second-hand toys or ones made by our dads or granddads. This is okay because most of them are very good at this and many a garden shed echoes to the sounds of banging and sawing in the lead up to this exciting day. Children are kept right away and not allowed at any time to go into the sheds. Imagine the joy and surprise when, on Christmas morning, boys find things like sailing ships and aeroplanes carved from wood, while the girls get doll's houses. Mums and grannies knit using wool saved up through the year, making us all socks, cardigans and jumpers. They also make clothes for their daughters' dolls.

So Christmas morning is just as exciting as it was before, because we refuse to let one man who has started a war spoil it for us. It was funny, really, because both our side and theirs stop the bombing from Christmas Eve until 27 December that year (1940), but we are all cramped into the shelters just the same. At least it was quiet though. But on 29 December London suffers a terrible raid, and much of it was on fire. Our teachers tell us afterwards that this raid is now being called the Second Great Fire of London.

On the platforms of the London Underground children can really enjoy themselves because they can have a full-sized tree and all of them take turns at decorating it. The porters and lady volunteers bring round drinks and small cakes and on Christmas morning the entire Underground network resounded to the shouts and screams of excitement as kids open their presents. Then, Germans or no Germans, we all do what we've done so far in our lives and get outside and play with our new toys. Boys revel in the fact they may have got a wooden ship or plane and they rush around with these. The rest of us, mimicking the enemy, shoot at them trying to bring the plane down or sink the ship. We don't succeed, of course, because the ship or plane is British so the Germans can't hit it, can they?

Girls are out too with their new skipping ropes and some of them have got new dolls – well, second-hand ones anyway. Their mums have knitted new clothes for the dolls they already have and the girls walk around, pushing their rickety prams to show these

The London Underground around Christmas time. Ladies brought around delicious cakes and sandwiches for the families sheltering from the bombs. (London Transport Museum)

Whether he is wearing his traditional red costume or the uniform of a
London Transport employee, the presents in Father Christmas's sack were
just as eagerly accepted by the children. (London Transport Museum)

off. They get right in our way and we shout at them to clear off or get back on the pavement out of the way of the battle that's going on in the middle of the street. The girls take no notice so we have to put up with this intrusion into our fight with the Germans. We find out later that these cheeky girls do this on purpose just to get in our way and be a nuisance. They laugh at us because all they can see are a lot of boys chasing each other with different-sized bits of wood. What a nerve. These bits of wood, as they call them, are weapons: swords, bows and arrows or guns. Surely they can work this out by the shouts we all give as battle commences. They have no imagination, though, so of course they will never understand us at all.

The lucky girls have found that their dads or grand-dads have made a doll's house for them and this makes not only them but also their friends so excited. They can put home-made furniture inside the house, and play for hours with it. This is alright for them, but boys need excitement too, and if even one boy in your road has been lucky enough to find a pair of roller skates at the bottom of his bed on Christmas morning then we all line up and take turns using them. There's never any argument over this and each boy gets his turn. Even the owner of the skates understands this and he waits to have a go along with the rest of us.

One thing stands out on this magical day and that's the bag or small stocking that most of us find with our presents. Inside this are treats none of us get during the year. Opening it is wonderful because you may find things like an orange, some nuts, a small bag of marbles, some plasticine and, wonder of wonders, a whole bar of chocolate. This is magic, because that entire bar is just for you. It doesn't have to be shared with your brothers and sisters because they've all got one in their stocking as well. Although we sometimes get chocolate during the year this always has to be shared out, either with your family or your friends. But this bar is all yours and we take full advantage of that. It's just like being in wonderland as you hold that chocolate in your hands. Once the wrapper is undone the chocolate disappears with a speed that dazzles.

Mums listen to the wireless and ladies like Gert and Daisy (Elsie Waters, 1893–1990 and Doris Waters 1904–78) give them tips on how to manage when things are in short supply. Marzipan for the cakes was being made with semolina and water with almond flavouring. Pudding mixture was made up with carrots and potatoes, along with the dried fruit that had been saved during the year. These both looked just as good as what we had before the war, and tasted pretty good as well. Silver sixpenny bits were put into the mixture and we loved to find one in our bit of pudding. Programmes on the wireless (*Workers' Playtime* 1941–64) describe how to serve up things like murkey. This is a substitute for turkey, mutton filled with home-made stuffing made mostly from breadcrumbs. It was make do and mend, and we all chipped in to make sure Christmas went with a bang – and not one that was caused by any bombs.

Mums have saved their coupons through the year to be able to get us extra food treats. They have saved sugar, margarine and dried fruit so that a Christmas cake can be made. Although the marzipan is home-made, and the mixture for the cake doesn't have any eggs in it, it still tastes great to us, because having a whole cake is a huge treat for the whole family. We don't know how our mums have managed to do this, but our sisters do because they helped with the baking. They may smirk at us because they know something that we don't, but we aren't worried about that – eating the cake is all we're interested in.

For some reason that none of us understand, icing sugar is banned in 1942, so mums have to find a way of making the icing to go on top of the cake. The icing was made by boiling granulated sugar, then mixing self-raising flour with that. It looks just the same as ordinary icing, though it tastes a bit funny. Some boys got their sisters to talk, so that's how we found out about this phoney icing. Small cakes appear as well, just like magic, and we get fruit and nuts too.

Some of us have older sisters who got married before their husbands went off to fight in the war. When we went to the wedding and looked at the wonderful cake that had three tiers to it, we all sat with our mouths watering just at the thought of getting a piece of it. With three tiers there was more than enough to go round so we should all get some. This cake didn't have home-made icing on it. In fact it didn't have any at all, our mums telling us that all the tiers were made of cardboard. The top one had a lid to it and when this was opened a small sponge cake was inside – another swizz, and all the fault of that Hitler bloke.

The meat we have for our wonderful, out of this world dinner on Christmas day was also something mums had to save up for. Most of them can't afford the price of a turkey, so they get us a chicken instead, and it takes a whole week's ration of coupons and a lot of money to bring it to the table.

Some families are lucky because they have chickens or rabbits in their back gardens. These are killed and are eaten for the dinner on Christmas day. Children have to be told a story to explain where they go late in December. A lot of them consider animals, especially rabbits and even chickens, as pets, so this disappear-ance would otherwise cause a great deal of upset. The usual explanation is that they have escaped. It's strange they never link this to the dinner placed before them with the home-produced meat as the crowning glory on the plate.

For children who were evacuated, this time of year is even more wonderful than any they have had at home. Life in towns and cities is hard, and dads have to work long hours to get enough money to look after us. But if children were lucky enough to be on a farm out in the country, they not only learnt about the animals but where things like milk and eggs really come from. They have such a great Christmas. Their mums send pocket money as well as things that have been made for them at home and on Christmas morning these are found under the big, home-grown tree in the lovely warm farmhouse lounge.

They get things like cream that we never even see let alone get, and many farms have orchards, so fresh fruit is available in the autumn. Farmers keep this in their barns and some of it is there for everyone to enjoy on that special day. Not all of them are as lucky as this, and many have to make do with whatever their adopted parents can provide for them, just the same as we do. But at least they have Christmas indoors and not cramped in an air-raid shelter.

The young ones don't really know what this time of year is all about, so when it's spent in the shelters a lot of them don't even notice anything different. But for us, war or no war, we make the best of it and go as close as we can to the way it was before all this began.

At school we all take part in the Nativity play, where the birth of Jesus in a stable in Bethlehem is played out to our mums and grannies. Wearing shepherds' costumes is a bit embarrassing, they look like ladies dresses, but as we're all wearing them it's not so bad. Then we break up, with our teachers always telling us not to eat too much Christmas pudding.

We all love books and look forward to getting at least one in our stocking. Adventure comics and books show boys like us having a great time and getting into all sorts of mischief, comics like *The Boys' Own Paper* being among the most popular. We love it if we find the annual with the rest of our presents. Girls liked soppy books and one they all talked about was by an author called Enid Blyton (1897–1949). She wrote about a girl's boarding school called St Clare's and girls up and down the country simply loved reading about this place. We aren't the least bit interested in these, of course, because boys aren't bothered what girls get up to, or about boarding schools in general.

The first book came out in 1941 and was called *The Twins at St Clare's*. Many girls find a copy of this with their presents. They get one every year afterwards as well because Enid Blyton wrote many more stories about this school, right up until 1945. These included *The O'Sullivan Twins* (1942), *Summer Term at St Clare's* (1943), *Claudine at St Clare's* (1944) and *Fifth Formers at St Clare's* (1945). These are good books really. Some of us even have a peek at our sisters' copies because they keep on about them so much. The girls in these stories did get up to a lot of things that most of us would like to have done. They play a game called lacrosse, which uses a small net on the end of a stick. None of us have a clue what this game is because we've never even heard of it. Enid Blyton then began another boarding school series called Mallory Towers, and these kept our girls supplied with exciting reading for the rest of the decade. Amongst these were *The First Term at Mallory Towers* (1946), *Second Form at Mallory Towers* (1947), *Third Year at Mallory Towers* (1948) and *Upper Fourth at Mallory Towers* (1949).

So what about us? The girls were well supplied with books by this author who was familiar to all of us from a young age when our parents read her Noddy books to us. Enid Blyton didn't let us down. In 1942 we get the first of the Famous Five books. Julian, Dick, George, Ann and Timmy the dog go off on their school holidays and have the most wonderful adventures catching crooks that the police haven't been able to find. It's smashing stuff, though we can't understand the character of George. She's a girl who wants to be a boy and so she dresses and acts like one all the time. It's funny to see a girl wearing a shirt and pullover with short trousers the same as us.

But the books are great and most of us look eagerly towards the bottom of our beds, in the shelter or after the war, in our own beds at home, to see if we have the latest exciting adventure. The first of these was called *Five on a Treasure Island* (1942), then we got *Five Go Adventuring Again* (1943), *Five Run Away Together*

(1944), *Five Go to Smuggler's Top* (1945), *Five Go Off in a Caravan* (1946) *Five on Kirrin Island Again* (1947), *Five Go off to Camp* (1948) and *Five Get into Trouble* (1949). Younger children have the Faraway Tree Stories read to them as well.

We like these books so much because all of us would just love to be out in the country having these sorts of adventures. Girls read them as well and get the same thrill as us. We play games taking turns to be members of the Famous Five.

The war with Germany may have brought us problems, both during and after, but one thing has come from it: it showed the world that British people can, and do, manage through whatever hardships are thrown at us. Adolf Hitler may have been the cause of these hardships but he, like others before him, didn't manage to beat us. Christmas carries on through it all and we carry on enjoying it.

Ten

MEMORABLE 1940S EVENTS

No one can talk about the 1940s without mentioning the Second World War. Parents, grandparents and children up and down the whole of the British Isles have all been through the fear and sometimes excitement of those five years of bombing and destruction – the food and clothing shortages, the rationing, and the boys who ride bicycles and bring telegrams to mums, causing them to break down in tears when they read them. They bring news that someone, a dad, an older brother, or even an uncle, who was away fighting the war has been killed in action and will never come home again.

But we enjoy the best bits, when our side wins battles and that Hitler bloke is beaten at last. He killed himself before the Allied armies took Berlin, and his country surrenders to us on 8 May 1945. Before this we have already had the joy of our men being rescued from Dunkirk, then the big desert victory at El Alamein to cheer about.

But it isn't all fun, even for us, because we hear stories of children our own age being killed when shelters took a direct hit from a German bomb. This was so sad and also so unbelievable. Children our age don't get killed. Only old granddads and grandmothers die don't they? We all live for at least a hundred years, so how could this happen to boys and girls the same age as us? We even hear of some evacuated children in a safe part of the country being strafed by a lone German plane and at least two of them got killed. Our parents swore when they heard this news, and what they said they would do to any German pilot who had to bail out and land in our towns frightens even us.

On Pathé News we are shown some of the experimental weapons that have been developed for our side to use in the war, and boy do we laugh when we watch this. There are some really funny things that should have worked but didn't. The ones that did, though, were out of this world.

The Dam Busters

There was the marvellous bouncing bomb that 617 Squadron, under Wing Commander Guy Gibson

(1918–44), used to burst the German dams and flood the area that was turning out war stuff. We are thrilled when we are told about this raid, which destroyed both the Mohne and Eder dams. They were hit by a bouncing bomb that was designed to bounce across the surface of the water then sink to the bottom of the dam wall before exploding. The bomb was dropped at very low altitude and Guy Gibson was awarded the Victoria Cross because the raid was so dangerous.

The bomb itself was designed by a man named Barnes Wallis (1887–1979). It fascinates us because we had been bouncing stones across water for ages. In rivers, even big ones like the Thames in London, or over the surface of lakes, boys would take flat stones and throw them low over the water. When they hit, they bounced quite a few times before stopping and sinking. Mr Wallis made a bomb that would rotate backwards at speed and do the same thing as our stones, bouncing across the water before hitting their target.

The grown-ups say this was such a thrilling thing for our RAF to have done that they ought to make a film about it. Sure enough, *The Dam Busters*, starring Richard Todd and Michael Redgrave, would come out in 1955.

The X-Craft

Another of our great inventions was the miniature submarine, called an X-Craft. This tiny sub carried a crew of four and it was so small they hardly had room to move. But the X-Craft were used to cripple Germany's biggest and most powerful battleship, the *Tirpitz*. Our navy had already fooled the pocket battleship *Graf Spee* and caused her to scuttle herself, then engaged and sunk the mighty *Bismarck* after crippling her with a torpedo hit to the rudder.

But *Tirpitz* was still a huge threat to our convoys. If she got out into the Atlantic our side would be in trouble because many more ships that were bringing us badly needed supplies would be sunk by its guns. Everyone knew this ship had to be stopped. She was holed up in a fjord in Norway and our navy had to find a way of sinking her or somehow stopping her from sailing out into the ocean. She was guarded by nets so normal size submarines couldn't get in, and our planes didn't have a heavy enough bomb to drop in order to cripple her.

So a plan was put into operation in September 1943. Six of these X-Craft submarines would be towed across to where the *Tirpitz* was. Another crew would take over from the ones who had crossed in the midgets and these would sneak up on the German ship and drop cargoes of high explosives right under the hull of the battleship. It worked but four of the X-Craft didn't make it to where the *Tirpitz* was and only two managed to lay their charges. The crews were taken prisoner after scuttling their crafts and were actually on board the *Tirpitz* when it exploded. Much damage was done to the battleship and she was laid up for repairs until well into 1944.

We all shout out loud when we hear that 617 Squadron had been given the job of attacking the *Tirpitz*. After more than one attempt they managed to drop a tallboy – another bomb invented by Barnes Wallis – from a long way up. It went through her decks and she turned over in the waters of the fjord. Our teachers said she never actually fired any of her guns at any of our ships, either merchant or Royal Navy.

Our brilliant navy began to win the Battle of the Atlantic with a device called Aztec on the bottom of our warships. This sent a radio signal through the water and it bounced off anything that was there. If the signal kept coming back even though the ship was going at full speed on the surface, it meant the echo was bouncing off the hull of a submarine, so then our ships would drop depth charges to destroy the enemy. It took a long time but we won in the end.

The allies managed to sink some of the other big ships of the German Navy, the *Scharnhorst* (26 December 1943) and the *Gneisenau*. None of

us can even pronounce this, but she was badly damaged by our air force in 1942 and never fought again
after that.

Then in June 1944, we all have such a thrill as
we watch the build up to D-Day in places like
Southampton, Portsmouth, and Plymouth. All sorts of
craft were in these ports, and when they sailed and
took on the Germans who were occupying countries
like France, Holland and Belgium our mums are over
the moon because they knew this meant the end of
the war was in sight.

So it was. What joy we have in May 1945 when
Germany surrenders and we have won. We were
now safe from bombing. Pathé News showed King
George VI with Queen Elizabeth together on the balcony of Buckingham Palace with our Prime Minister
Winston Churchill and his wife waving to the crowd
in Trafalgar Square and Mr Churchill giving his V for
victory sign.

The war between America and Japan took a bit
longer and was brought to an end by America dropping two atomic bombs on cities in Japan. We have no
idea what an atomic bomb is, but our teachers tell us
they are so powerful that just one can destroy a whole
town or city. We are told it is a good job Hitler never
got one of them to use against us because we would
have lost the war if he had.

There was a story about somewhere in Norway where the Germans had workers making heavy water, which is needed to make atom bombs. But this never got to Germany because the brave men of the Norwegian Underground sank the ferry that was carrying it. This was an amazing thing for them to do and made sure that Germany never got such an awful weapon. What puzzles us is heavy water. Why did they need a factory to produce this? We all know how heavy water is when there's a lot of it in one washing up bowl. And when we have to empty the tin bath down the outside drain our mums are always saying how heavy the water is inside it, so why all the fuss about heavy water in a foreign country?

Now with the war over we welcome back friends who have been evacuated and introduce them to our camps in bombed-out houses. They, like us, now watch as emergency housing is put up for the families who had been bombed out to live in. They are prefabs and they are very comfortable inside. We also watch as builders start to clear bombsites and build real houses and some of the younger children play in the cement mixers in the evenings. Their mums would have a fit if they knew because this is a very dangerous thing to do.

But other things are happening as well, besides fathers coming home and sport returning. Bonfire

Night is back and so is the right to make up a guy, using old clothes stuffed with paper and any old rags our mothers will let us have. This goes on top of the bonfire on that magical night, 5 November. We all get back into the habit of racing out with our guys and picking the best spots to parade them, while politely asking passing grown-ups, 'Penny for the guy, please?' Most of them happily give this to us so we end up with a super lot of money to spend on sweets and stuff. Our parents buy the fireworks for us – these come back into the shops in 1946 – and our dads light the bonfires we have spent weeks collecting stuff for and building up.

We are all very good at this, collecting paper and anything else that would burn, because we did it before the war, and even during, when we collected waste stuff for the war effort. But now, once again this collecting is done for our own benefit. Now the explosions and fires that light up the night are not caused by bombs but by fireworks. Potatoes are baked by sticking a wooden stake in them and placing them into the bonfire. We eat them as they came out, all black and sooty, but blinking lovely. Everything is watched over by our newly returned dads. And we never put a foot wrong on this day either, getting our hands on bangers and throwing them around, using them as our own bombs. Would we do such a thing?

ABC Minors

Around 1946 another wondrous thing happens: the start of the ABC Minors. Most big ABC picture houses all over the country, which we called either the fleapit (Regal) or the cabbage (Savoy), are involved. It starts with kids aged 5 to 15 queuing to get our membership cards and ABC Minors badge. Then, on the first Saturday, all cinemas that are doing ABC Minors are packed out with boys and girls who were there to have a really great time watching the films we all love.

We relish the excitement of a weekly serial such as Flash Gordon or our favourite secret agent, Dick Barton. They always got into such awful situations where they were surely going to be killed. But next week we are shown how they escaped just in time and were able to go after the crooks again. This is mainly boy's stuff, of course, but the girls seem to like it as well – well they cheered as loudly as us when our heroes escaped every week. The cost to get into the Minors is 6*d*, but some only pay 1*d* as they bring an empty jam jar with them and give this to the lady in the ticket office. We scoffed at that because now the war is over getting 6*d* is easy-peasy. Just run some errands for our mums or other ladies in your road at 3*d* a time and the Minor's money, as well as some for sweets, is earned.

The morning began with the cinema manager, usually known to us as Uncle John, coming on stage and saying, 'Good morning children. We will now sing the Minors song.' The words of this were put up on to the screen and then the tune, 'Blaze Away' by Abe Holzmann (1874–1939), started up and we all sang the song together. One of the lines from this was 'we're all pals together'. Really? No, we're flipping well not!

Every Saturday morning in cinemas up and down the country World War Three takes place. Catapults, peashooters and even pieces of elastic are used to propel missiles, usually dried peas, all around to hit as many kids as possible, boys as well as girls. And we have to put up with these being shot back at us too. It's alright if a boy you have just hit shoots back and gets you. But if it's a girl, well, the embarrassment is huge.

Sometimes the cinema staff tell us we will all now sing songs they call 'patriotic'. What on earth does that mean? But we sing all the usual things, like 'There'll always be an England'. Then if the noise level goes up too much the picture is stopped and we are shouted at from the stage to quieten down or else we will all be thrown out. It never works, of course, because making a noise is what we do all the time and we're pretty good at it.

Children whose birthdays come in the week before the Minors, or on the same day, are invited up on to the stage where they are given a card and some ice cream from the cinema staff. Then all the others sing 'Happy Birthday' to them. Some kids go up more than once, some doing it at least five times a year. Well, the staff can't keep up to date with every child who comes each week can they? This is, of course, against the rules, so we don't do it. It's just that most of us have got at least three birthdays a year, you see.

The Royal Wedding

In 1947 our mums, grannies and older sisters start getting excited about the news on the wireless and in the papers. The engagement in July of the king's eldest daughter, Princess Elizabeth, to Prince Philip of Greece and Denmark, who they all say is so handsome, had been announced. The wedding is set for November and will be in Westminster Abbey. All of the women are now chattering over garden fences, wondering what the princess will be wearing on the big day. What a silly question. Even us boys know she will be wearing a wedding dress, so why all the mystery? The papers say she will have eight bridesmaids who will be led by her younger sister, Princess Margaret; the girls at school are all drooling about this and wishing they could be one of these. Our sympathies, though, are with the two pageboys. None of us would want to be out in public dressed like that. We've all seen pageboys before and they look just like Little Lord Fauntleroy!

On the day before the wedding people who have come from all over the country, including Scotland and Wales, are camping out on the streets to get a good look at the royals as they go past on their way to the abbey. None of them are worried about sleeping out in the open like this, as so many had to do it in the war. Not even the wet weather on the day causes any trouble because they are all so excited.

As the royal couple, now married, come out of the abbey there is a deafening roar from the crowd. The princess is wearing a wedding dress, just like we knew she would, but our mums and sisters are still saying how wonderful it is and how lovely she looks in it. Well we can't argue with that because we think so too, though none of us would ever actually say so. The roars from the crowd last all the way up the Mall to the palace. Then crowds rush forward and gathered outside the gates and cheer their heads off as the couple, along with the king and queen and members of the royal family appear on the balcony of Buckingham Palace.

We had to wait to see this on Pathé News and when we did it wasn't just the girls who were excited. We all thought our princess looked super so we cheered at the screen as loudly as any of them. The whole royal family looked grand up there – even the two pageboys!

Laurel and Hardy

The year 1947 is such an exciting one. So much happens and one thing event in particular we can hardly believe. Our big comedy heroes, who we laugh so much at each week at the Minors, are actually coming here, to our country. Yes, Stan Laurel and Oliver Hardy are going to tour all over the place and the lucky ones

Stan Laurel and Oliver Hardy delighted so many people, adults as well as children, when they toured Britain in 1947. Here the duo is seen at the reopening of the Romney, Hythe & Dimchurch Railway. (Romney, Hythe & Dimchurch Railway)

will get the chance of a lifetime to meet them. Wow, what a great thing that will be!

Many families, with their children jumping up and down, watch these two great men as they arrive on board the liner *Queen Elizabeth* after it docked at Southampton. This is all on Pathé News of course and the noise inside the fleapits when this is shown is even louder than we make each Saturday morning. From Southampton they go to places like Portsmouth and Brighton, then down into Kent where they attend the reopening of the Romney, Hythe & Dimchurch Railway. In London they appear at the Palladium, then at seaside towns like Skegness, Morecombe, Tynemouth and Blackpool, to name just a few. In Scotland they perform at the Glasgow Empire and in Edinburgh and draw really large crowds.

To have your chance to see them, even from a distance is just like a miracle because it is really them in person and not a picture up on the screen.

Kon-Tiki

Something else happens in 1947 that catches the attention of the whole country: the amazing story of the Kon-Tiki expedition. Some men from Norway have built a super raft and sailed it across the Pacific Ocean from South America to the Pacific Islands

(Tuamotu Islands), wherever they are. The leader is a man called Thor Heyerdahl and he set off on this raft with five other men in his crew. It is supposed to show that people in the olden days could have built rafts and travelled to other countries on them. That they travelled over a thousand miles on a raft has become world news and just about every school in this country knows about it. A film is made that comes out in 1950 and we make sure we see this as well.

Now, we British boys and girls have been making our own rafts for yonks, but hearing about this famous voyage a new wave of raft-building begins all over the country. The great Kon-Tiki challenge was well and truly on. Trees that were blown up by German bombs are lashed together to make our own version. We know Mr Heyerdahl and his men used large trunks of Balsa wood for their raft, but we can't get any of that. We haven't even heard of it! We make do, as all British kids will, and use what we have available. The girls want to be in on the act too, so we have them making the sails. When everything is done and the raft, which looks so sturdy on the bank, is ready for launching we let the girls smash the lemonade bottle on it. The mighty *Titanic* didn't look any better than our rafts when she was launched. We are proud to see our efforts now out on the water and ready, as were we, for the big adventure ahead. Now at least six boys jump aboard and another Kon-Tiki expedition could begin.

Once underway, though, the current takes the raft downstream and things start to go wrong. The raft looked alright before, but now it starts to behave in a most alarming fashion. It won't steer for a start, and our knots aren't nearly as good as they should have been. Gradually at first, the tree trunks beneath us begin to move until, with a horrid groaning noise, they simply tear apart, dumping the whole lot of us in the water. It's a good job we're all used to swimming with our clothes on. The girls were no help either; they split their sides laughing at us as we drag ourselves out of the water and splosh our way home. Houses all over the country resound to the sounds of mothers shouting at their sons then clouting them round the ears for coming home in such a state.

Thor Heyerdahl and his crew may have sailed for a thousand miles, but I believe the average British boy's expedition was a maximum of one mile before disaster struck. This isn't the way it always happens, though. The Boy Scouts and the Sea Scouts know how to build rafts properly, so all of them are alright out on the water.

The Olympic Games

In 1948 the Olympic Games start again. It is the first time they had been staged since 1936. And boy are we all excited because it is being put on right here in our country. The 1948 Olympics are in our capital city of London, and they are opened by King George VI. The main area for the athletics is Wembley Stadium and athletes from all over the world come here to compete. There are lots of other sports as well, of course, and we are hoping Britain will win a load of medals.

Some of our more affluent relatives and neighbours have television in their homes by this time and they watch some of the Games on them. It is the first time television has been filmed as an outside broadcast. Most of us have to wait to watch this amazing thing on Pathé News at the cinema. It is exciting. Britain wins three gold medals in the rowing events and sailing; fourteen silver medals in athletics, boxing, cycling, hockey and weightlifting; and six bronze medals in athletics, cycling, equestrian and swimming.

Most of us do much better than our sports stars when we have sports days at school. We win far more races than they did. It isn't fair; we don't have our king watching us and then putting gold medals round our necks when we win. All we get is a pat on the back and a 'well done' from our mums. What a blinking swizz!

All in all the whole of the 1940s is a wonder to us, filled first with a mixture of fear and excitement, then we are able to enjoy Britain starting to recover. The sheer joy of just being British shines through for us all.

Eleven

WHATEVER HAPPENED TO?

Looking back at this remarkable decade in the history of this great country, it will always be a wonder to me that so many of us took things for granted. Women had to put up with so much hard work in order to keep their homes clean and tidy, and their children fed, washed and clothed. They did it every day with very little recognition.

The era was overshadowed by the extremely strict Victorian regime that had preceded it, and much of that culture was still in place. Men, when they were home from the war, were still the sole wage earner in most homes and as such were looked on as gods. Many of them, for instance, never sat down to their evening meal with the rest of their family, the children having been fed earlier. In homes up and down the country, the man sitting alone eating his meal was commonplace. Not all were like this, of course, and some fathers enjoyed eating while surrounded by their wife and children, but that strict ruling was lurking just under the surface. Children were seen and not heard.

It is incomprehensible now that we believed the utter rubbish we were told about anything to do with that taboo subject of sex. We accepted, without question, what our mothers and schoolteachers told us, because they were grown-up. They knew what they were talking about, and they wouldn't fib to us would they? We believed that babies were delivered by storks, which carried them in cloths in their beaks and left them in the cabbage patch in your back garden. There were at least two things wrong with this statement. Britain doesn't have any storks as native birds, so none of us had ever seen one. Where did they come from and where did they get the babies from? How did they know which gardens to leave the babies in? Secondly not all gardens had a cabbage patch. The practice of growing your own had been even more important during the hard times of the Second World War, so vegetables were grown a lot more then than before it started. Anderson shelters were still in use as garden sheds and a lot still had the vegetable patch on top of them. But what if cabbages were not being grown? Where would the stork leave the baby then? It beggars belief that we kids accepted stuff like this simply because grown-up people told us about them.

Women had very few, if any, labour-saving devices and had to do most jobs in the home by hand. The gas copper in the kitchen was the pivotal piece of equipment, providing all the hot water. After lighting the gas and waiting for the water inside to heat up, the family's washing could be boiled and got clean that way. But if collars and cuffs were really dirty – work shirts, especially – ladies then had to scrub these separately. To do this she used a washboard. This device was placed at one end of a bowl of water and the shirt was placed on to this. The collars and cuffs of this garment were then soaped and the offending parts rubbed against the ribbed surface. It was hard work but it did the job. These washboards were later used by young men who formed skiffle groups. They were held in the same position as when doing the washing, but in the skiffle group a teenage boy would rub his fingernails over this same surface and make an accompaniment to the tune being played. I wonder whatever happened to them?

Rinsing was also a chore, with a set of wooden tongs being used to get the washing out of the copper and into the sink. Once done and the washing rinsed there was the mammoth task of pegging it all out on to the line in the back garden. But of course, most of the water still held in the wet washing had to be squeezed out, and the mangle was used to do this. In back gardens all over this country, boys wrestled with the huge wheel that turned the rollers. It was so different from the inventions that followed when proper washing machines and smaller mangles, followed by spin and then tumble dryers, were introduced. Likewise, the flat irons that many women used were solid and had to be heated up on the gas stove before they could be used to do the family's ironing. They were clumsy and often dangerous, as they got so hot.

Inside the house, carpet sweepers were used, if there were any carpets, that is. They went backwards and forwards over the carpets or mats and picked up any dirt that was on them. This too was hard work and blooming noisy. Some well-off houses had things called vacuum cleaners that they plugged in. The dirt was then sucked inside a bag that hung down the front, which had to be emptied every so often. But in most homes mums got down on their hands and knees and polished the lino with Ronuck polish. This lino covered the wooden floorboards all over the house, upstairs and down, and this was something all of us took for granted. The days of wall-to-wall carpeting were still some distance into the future.

So too was wallpaper and emulsion paint. Wallpaper was available, but the average working man did not earn enough money each week to be able to afford a luxury like this. So walls and ceilings were painted by something we all knew as distemper. Dads mixed this dry powder with water in a bucket then painted it on the walls. It seemed to work alright, but the mixing and painting, done with brushes, took a long time to complete.

Bread was kept in an enamel bread bin that sat on the side of the sink, and perishable things like meat and bacon went into the meat safe outside the back door or in a shady part of the kitchen.

For most of us television was simply something that was out of our reach. Our parents would have needed to win the football pools to be able to afford one of those, so our entertainment came from the wireless. These sets were made of Bakelite and inside they had large glass tubes called valves that made the set work. Our whole world at home revolved around the wireless, and families listened together in the evenings to such programmes as *Children's Hour* and in the afternoons it was *Listen with Mother*. These sets now are antiques, but in the 1940s they were an everyday piece of equipment.

We had another way to listen to music and that was by playing records. These were round plastic things that you had to handle carefully, because if you dropped them they were liable to break. They were placed on the turntable of a gramophone and when they were spun they went round seventy-eight times a minute (78rpm). You took the metal arm that was bent back and turned it the right way round before placing the big needle on to the record. We never knew how the music came out of the speakers, but many of us had one of these in our house. The problem was they had to be wound up. A handle for this was on the side of the gramophone. Once fully wound the motor worked really well and the record played properly. But if any of us forgot to wind the thing up, the record would suddenly slow down as the motor began to die. The result was a horrible low, groaning noise that just moments before had been a man or a lady singing. One of us would hurriedly turn the handle so that the record started playing as it should again. They were pretty primitive, I suppose, but at least they didn't have a great big horn sticking out of them like our grandparents used to have on theirs in the olden days.

Some posh people had telephones in their houses so that they could ring people like their friends or the doctor. These were supplied by the post office and were small black things that usually stood on a table in the hall of their homes. But for most of us there was only the one telephone box that had to be shared by a whole load of roads. Calls from these cost tuppence (2*d*), which was put into the slot. Then, when the number you dialled is answered, you press button A before you can speak to the person on the other end of the phone. If no one answers then you press button B in order to get your money back.

There was another type of phone box, but these aren't to be used by members of the public because they are police boxes. Some of these are small black boxes set into walls, while others are sited on a pole, something like a small lamppost. These were connected to police stations as well as other emergency services. They were usually set up at the end of roads and they were for the sole use of policemen out on their beats. These men called in to the stations to let their sergeants know that things are alright on their particular beat. Or in the case of emergency, when more policemen were needed because a crime is being committed or a bad accident has happened, the call was again put through from one of these police phone boxes. The other method policemen used to call for help was the whistle. The sound of this rending the air around always made us so excited, because it was just like the films we saw when the crooks were being chased and the policemen were all blowing their whistles to let the other cops know where the crooks were. The best film showing this came out in 1950. It was called *The Blue Lamp*. PC Dixon, played by Jack Warner (1895-1981), is shot by a man played by Dirk Bogarde (1921–99), who then goes on the run, and police whistles were sounding all over the place. We sometimes played our rough-and-tumble games in fields where there were police boxes in plain view, and when the local bobby

A police constable about to use the police phone at the special call box.
(Hampshire Constabulary History Society)

turns up to make a call we suddenly became the best-behaved kids in the country.

Directing traffic was another duty for policemen and when on this they had white armlets that went from their wrists to their elbows. This was to make sure people driving cars, lorries or horse-drawn carts could see them and stop when indicated. He would do this by holding up his right arm to them. Then he would turn and look at the traffic coming in the opposite direction and wave them on. These policemen also held up the traffic when we needed to cross the roads, and woe betide us if we moved to cross before he told us too.

Very few cars were on the roads and most of the ones we saw were black Fords and Austin Sevens. It was towards the end of the 1940s that we saw much more modern cars like Ford Zephyrs, with two-tone tyres. A much more ordinary sight was the horse and cart. Apart from the money-making practice of scooping up the manure from these animals, it was great if we could get permission to ride on the carts, just like our cowboy heroes in the films we watched. If our mums would let us we gave the horses a slice of bread, and they loved that.

Houses were always filled with flies and other insects in the summer and mums everywhere would have loved to be able to get rid of these pests. We had flypapers hanging up all over the place and though some flies did stick, most of the others in the house stayed there and got on to all of the food. Then an advert that appeared in the papers for a device that could trap these pesky insects. Some people sent off for one of them, paying a shilling and then waiting for this marvellous device to be sent back to them through the post. What a swizz it was. People received two small blocks of wood labelled block A and block B and a small instruction leaflet. Take block A in your right hand, then entice your flies, beetles and bugs on to this. Then taking block B in your left hand, bring this smartly down on top of block A. Even mums said words we hadn't heard before when they saw how they had been cheated out of their precious money in this way.

Steam trains were the main way to travel between towns and cities, but journeys within your own town were mostly made by tram. These clattered along on rails with power coming from an overhead cable. A long arm was on top of the trams and this connected with the overhead wire. The seats on these were all made of wood and weren't that comfortable. In the summer it was great to go upstairs on a tram, especially if it was an open-topped one, though if it started raining it wasn't half as much fun. The trams were driven by men who stood at the front and turned two handles that controlled the speed. They didn't have to steer because the trams went where the rails took them.

There was a conductor who came round taking the fares that our mothers paid and they gave her tickets for this. Most of us claimed these for our collections.

Fire extinguishers in the home weren't even heard of, so some of us had a stirrup pump. The London fire brigade had some of these as well and they were sometimes used to put out fires. These things stood in a bucket of water and they had a pump that went up and down and forced the water to go through a rubber tube, and from there the jet of water was directed on to the fire. There was a foot pedal that you had to stand on to stop them coming out of the bucket as you pumped the handle. Extinguishers did exist, of course, and we had some at school, but many houses simply relied on the stirrup pump instead.

There were some more modern houses that actually had a bathroom inside. What a luxury this was. People who had one of these had a bath in the room as well as a basin for washing hands and cleaning your teeth. They still had an outside toilet. In the bathroom, at one end of the bath, was a water heater called a geyser. To light one of these you had to be very careful and we kids made sure we were well out of the way when our mum did this. There was a tap outside this device, which was turned on. This meant gas was now coming out of the burner at the end of a small metal arm. It also meant gas was coming out of the ring inside the geyser. A match was used

Trams, like these in Southampton, were the most common means of getting around in the 1940s. (Project 57 Southampton)

to light the burner at the end of the small arm, then this was swung under the geyser and this in turn lit the gas ring and started heating the water inside. But when that ring did ignite it did so with an enormous bang that sent us scurrying away to hide every time. It always seemed such a big chore for the little trickle of hot water that came running out the copper spout to fill in the bath, and it took ages. But it sure beat filling a tin bath then having to empty this down the outside drain.

We had rubber hot water bottles that our mums put in our beds every night in the winter. The grown-ups used china ones that had a stopper in the middle that had to be taken out before this clumsy-looking thing could be filled with hot water.

Kitchen ranges have disappeared but they were commonplace in the 1940s. Although they only had a small grate, the heat given out from the fire inside was very good indeed, and the oven that was next to the grate could be used for baking. They had a very narrow metal pipe that took the smoke from the fire and sent it through to the main chimney, and from there out into the open air. Many a child stood gazing at this as Christmas came around and tried to work out how a man as big as Father Christmas could get through such a narrow space and then out the tiny opening behind the grill of the grate.

Many toys are no longer around. Some children had marble shooters. These looked just like a real gun but they shot marbles out instead, and boys used these when playing allies in the gutters. Most of us didn't even see one of these things and we would have scoffed at them if we did. None of us needed a gun to shoot our marbles. We were experts at doing this with our hands. Catapults were handmade, taking wood and then shaping it into a Y before stretching elastic across the top. These were used with devastating effect to shoot things like dried peas at each other.

Besides soapbox carts and bicycles, we made our own weapons for playing, and these included guns. A piece of wood was shaped to resemble this and the firing noise shouted by the boy using it. Bows were made from short, thin branches and skilfully bent with a string stretched tight between the ends. Arrows were also made from thin strips of wood then used with skill when fired at the enemy. We were all excellent shots when using these weapons and were in fact better than our film star cowboys. We could also outshoot Robin Hood anytime with our own version of the long bow. But the other side always cheated when you shot them at point-blank range or hit them with your spear or arrows. They simply brushed this aside and kept coming at you. Your shout of, 'Hey you're dead. I just shot you,' was answered by, 'No I'm not. You missed!'

To our great delight, footballs were sometimes found at the end of our beds at Christmas. These were made of leather and had a rubber inner tube. Before they could be played with in the streets it was necessary to ask your dad, or a neighbour, to use a bicycle pump to fill these tubes. Then the ball was laced shut so another great game of football could be played in the road, which England always won, of course. These balls were smashing to play with when they were dry, but once out in wet weather the leather got really heavy and they soon resembled cannonballs. Anyone who had football boots was really lucky. These had big leather studs on the bottom and came up over the ankles. Long laces went right round the top then down under the instep as well, before coming back up and tying at the top. It wasn't a good idea to let

This poster shows the bulldog spirit of British boys, willing to help in any way they could to beat the aggressor from Germany. (Brooklands Museum)

these boots get wet either, because the same thing happened to them as the balls. They weighed a ton and running in them was nearly impossible.

Home-made toys, the hard work of our mothers, harsh school life and all the rationing and shortages made up the life all of us went through and will never forget. Because it was difficult, we proved that children have the sort of resilience to face anything that comes their way and simply go on with the business of being kids. The bulldog spirit instilled in each and every one of us kept us in such great spirits that a man called Adolf Hitler, who caused such damage and loss of life in so many countries, failed to dent.

British children defied him. We lived through the most troubled decade in our country's history with determination and high spirits. We laughed and played in the streets and bombed-out buildings and went about our lives in our own way, through it all managing to have fun. So, long live the British spirit and may many more children from Great Britain live their lives too in this wonderful country we all call home.